Wars of the Theatres:
The Poetics of Personation in
the Age of Jonson

MATTHEW STEGGLE

Wars of the Theatres: The Poetics of Personation in the Age of Jonson

English Literary Studies
University of Victoria
1998

ENGLISH LITERARY STUDIES
Published at the University of Victoria

ISBN 0-920604-57-9

The ELS Monograph Series is published in consultation with members of the Department by ENGLISH LITERARY STUDIES, Department of English, University of Victoria, P.O. Box 3070, Victoria, B.C., Canada, v8w 3w1.

ELS Monograph Series No. 75
© 1998 by Matthew Steggle

The cover shows the frontispiece of Q3 of *A Game at Chess* (1625), reproduced by kind permission of the Bodleian Library.

In Memoriam
Jeremy Jones
1967-1994

CONTENTS

ILLUSTRATIONS

ACKNOWLEDGMENTS

This monograph draws heavily on my doctoral thesis, the funding for which was provided by scholarships from the British Academy and from Trinity College, Oxford. I am very grateful to both these institutions.

I'd like to thank my supervisors at Oxford, John Carey, Terence Cave, and Tony Nuttall, for their collective learning, tact, and forbearance. I'd also like to thank Katherine Duncan-Jones and Richard Dutton, my examiners, for their advice and help, and for the surprising reference from Pliny. Discussions with Matthew Hansen, Matthew Woodcock, Helen Vincent, and Katharine Chubbuck have been important. Outside Britain, Bob Evans, Helen Ostovich, Jon Haarberg and Ton Hoenselaars have all shared their expertise freely, and it's a pleasure to be able to acknowledge their help.

Lastly, I'd like to thank my parents, and Lucy, Peter, Frazer, and Maddy; all at Trinity Archive; Adam Stephen, Charlotte Suthrell, and Dinah Birch; friends for retaining a sense of fun; and Clare, for many things including being more important than Ben Jonson.

INTRODUCTION

This study considers as a genre satirical comedies of the English Renaissance that represent living people on stage. In this light, one can see these comedies situated at the fault lines of early professional drama, taking part not just in interpersonal conflicts but in crucial intellectual and practical struggles over the nature and future of that drama.

One of the reasons why no overall study of such "personation" has ever been done before is that the topic is—as far as possible—avoided by twentieth-century critics. In particular, study of personation has still not recovered from the damage done by the old view of Renaissance plays as biographical documents admitting of interpretations *à clef*. An excellent example of the effects of this method is provided by early criticism of Jonson's *Every Man Out of His Humour*, where rival Victorian "decipherings" of the play saw in it thinly veiled caricatures of late Elizabethan celebrities such as Gabriel Harvey, Sir Walter Raleigh, Anthony Munday and Sir John Harington. In many cases several equally plausible identifications can be offered for the same character, since Puntarvolo, for instance, was taken at various times to be a transparent disguise for each of the four men named above. Such criticism is unsubstantiated, reductive and naive, and in reaction most subsequent critics have avoided considering the whole area of personation as far as possible.[1]

However, the problem is that periodically such representation *does* happen, and *does* affect the play to which it belongs. Dekker and Middleton's *The Roaring Girl* is predicated upon its representation of a living person, Mary Frith. Middleton's *A Game at Chess* cannot be considered simply as an abstract allegory—its representation on stage of living people was what defined its contemporary appeal and notoriety. To take an extreme example, the eponymous lead character in the Red Bull comedy *Swetnam the Woman-hater, Arraigned by Women* evidently does have some significant connection with the Jacobean writer and prominent misogynist Joseph Swetnam—a connection so important that the play cannot properly be considered without reference to it.

Swetnam will be given full discussion in its place, but for the moment the play is worth brief consideration, as it offers a typical example of the paradoxes involved in the representation of living people on the English professional stage. In particular, there is the conundrum that personation is at once impossible and yet unavoidable. Impossible, since of course on one level no play can "bring someone on stage." The source

11

behind *Swetnam* is a Spanish novella in which a misogynist has an important plot function, and it might be argued that the anonymous English playwright has simply and opportunistically given this pre-existing character the name of Joseph Swetnam, a well-known contemporary writer against women. As a matter of fact, in the case of *Swetnam* one can show that the resemblances go much further than that, and that the play is specifically constructed around the representation of Joseph Swetnam; but all the same, it is undeniably true that the play's character called Swetnam is no indexical shadow of his model, but a character in a dramatic context.

On another level, it's equally impossible *not* to represent someone on stage. Apropos of *Swetnam*, for instance, Simon Shepherd has pointed out that the Sicilian royal family in this play bears a resemblance to that of King James I, in that there is an eldest son who has died, a daughter who is getting married, and a younger son who is preparing to assume his mantle as heir to the throne. On the basis of these similarities, Shepherd proceeds to show how the royal plot of the play may be read as a political allegory, complete with reference to the memory of Queen Elizabeth in the scenes where the younger son disguises himself as an Amazon.[2] This is an attractive idea, though chronologically awkward: the play itself was written between 1617 and 1619, years after the death of Prince Henry and the marriage of Princess Elizabeth. However, the parallels are there should one choose to apply them. More broadly still, it can be contended that any stage king in Jacobean drama is inevitably to some extent a representation of King James I. And such topical applications need not be confined to works written under James: as one seventeenth-century reader wrote of possible personal reference in *Volpone*, "Fancy hath made actions . . . and persons of a 1000 year standing to poynt at those of our own time imagining that the Actors of an old play resembled some of their new spectators."[3]

So in one sense personation is impossible, while at the same time it is inevitable. Between these two poles lies the area I want to look at, of deliberate and specific representation. For example, *Swetnam*'s central character, who will be referred to hereafter as Swetnam/Misogenos, often speaks in quotations from the real Swetnam's pamphlets, shares his interest in fencing, and is more than just a generic misogynist whose contemporary name is an afterthought. At the same time, the possible interpretations of the character are *limited*. The application is narrowed and made unavoidable in a way not true of broader parallels between the royal families of *Swetnam*'s Sicily and Joseph Swetnam's Britain. King Atticus may be in one sense of the word an allegorical "representation" of King James, indeed no proof could be offered that he isn't, but such representation functions in a mode different from that of Swetnam in Swetnam/Misogenos.

In this study, the focus is on highly specific representations like *Swetnam*'s version of Joseph Swetnam, and disputed claims of personal reference are avoided as far as possible. Most of the plays at the heart of this study happily advertise in their paratexts the personation which they contain. In the case of only one of the plays central to the discussion—Marston's *What You Will*—has there been any serious recent critical contention as to whether or not it does contain the personal reference ascribed to it here. Indeed, only by examining these plays as a genre, by considering the characteristic mechanics of personation where it is obvious, will it be possible to lay the foundations for investigation of more dubious examples.

A word about critical theory. In relating these works to a historical context, this study is certainly historicist, with a small *h*. To a certain extent, it is also New Historicist, for instance in its perception of history as a cultural construct rather than an objective phenomenon, and in its interrogation of the gaps and the absences in that history. However, this study avoids the characteristic rhetorical features associated with New Historicist writing, such as the use of anecdotal, marginal parables and deliberately recherché associative leaps, and aspires instead to more conventional scholarly values. In an area such as personation, concerning which one predecessor lamented that "A scholar who desires a reputation for sanity hardly dares touch the subject,"[4] careful demonstration of one's working is a necessity. In this respect this work is closest to the sort of historical and historicist research being undertaken by critics such as Richard Dutton and Robert C. Evans. Evans' work on Jonson and especially his concept of "micropolitics" are used extensively in what follows.[5]

Another of my central concerns is ultimately historicist in its agenda, namely, the way in which anachronisms can result from attempts to consider all Renaissance drama using a single model of what the plays might be. Jonson's belief that "plays" are "works," a belief which still conditions modern thinking about the literary status of seventeenth-century drama texts, is *not* self-evidently true; indeed, many of the plays considered in this study, notably *What You Will* and *Satiromastix*, are arguing quite cogently and intelligently against it—privileging performance at the expense of textuality. Hence the pointed choice of the phrase "the Age of Jonson" in my title, as the Age of Jonson is a

13

retrospective label, and the War of the Theatres demonstrates that it is false to assume that modern, broadly Jonsonian models of text and drama were shared at all by Jonson's colleagues.

Furthermore, "textuality" as a concept is open to interrogation. Terence Cave, for instance, describes a situation in sixteenth-century France where writers dislike the slippery uncertainties of textual discourse, striving instead to imitate the immediacy of the spoken.[6] For many seventeenth-century British dramatists, though, the reverse is the case, and text, both handwritten and printed, seems to represent a reassuring stability of meaning and authority noticeably lacking from performance on the stage. In personally satirical drama, where injudicious frankness was often associated with litigation and jail, professional writers must have found it relatively harder to entertain doubts about the possibility of correspondence between words and real life. Hence this study uses the word "textuality" to describe the fact of being in written form, the equivalent condition to "theatricality," rather than necessarily as an invocation of Derridean epistemological uncertainty. Indeed, one of the processes that one will see working through the plays described in this study is a problematisation of ideas about whether a professionally composed play is a textual phenomenon or a performance, and how one might locate meaning within it. Surprisingly, and consistently, personation is bound up with all these concerns.

On the surface, this is an odd claim. Why is personation so caught up in this one particular debate over the textual status of drama? And on which side of it does personation, as a technique, fall? The idea that personation acts as a device whereby one can bring discussion of drama into a drama itself is self-evidently true as regards those satirical plays whose victims are other playwrights. The roll-call of such playwright victims, as the following chapters will show, includes Jonson, Marston, Dekker, Munday, Chapman, Suckling, and Davenant. All are satirised not just as individuals, but with particular mocking reference to their own dramatic output. Another distinction shared by five of these seven writers, incidentally, is that they wrote personally satirical comedies themselves.

But furthermore, personation offers a degree of self-referentiality. It offers a window into considering the nature of the dramatic which one could call either metatheatrical or metatextual, though to make a choice which of the two terms one prefered would be to prejudge the issue at hand. Personation, in either case, breaks down normal barriers between text and context, or between stage and audience. In the hands of Ben Jonson, personation is a device eminently compatible with a view of drama as a textual phenomenon. It comes endorsed with classical precedent, most notably that of Aristophanes, and carried out—in *Poetaster*, for instance—within the confines of imitations of Horace buttressed by marginal annotations. Jonson uses personation to satirise both the ideas and the morals of contemporaries who disagree with him on this issue. But in the hands of Marston and Dekker, personation works in quite the opposite way, using quotations from Jonson's own works to mock the inadequacy of such a logocentric critical and ethical stance faced with the shifting uncertainties of a world that does not share it. This study traces the development and change in these battle-lines through satirical comedies from 1598 to 1640.

The scope of this project, then, is quite narrow. It is concerned with professional satirical comedies of the English Renaissance that represent living people on stage. Personally satirical masques such as *Time Vindicated*, apprentice plays such as *The Hog Hath Lost His Pearl*, and university plays such as *Pedantius* or *Club Law*, are therefore excluded despite the openly personal satire that they contain. Also excluded are professional tragedies, even though they often depicted heroes only recently deceased, and featured representations of other people still alive, for instance, Marlowe's *Massacre at Paris* (1593), Fletcher's *Sir John Van Olden Barnavelt* (1619), or Chapman's *The Conspiracy and Tragedy of Charles Duke of Byron* (1608). All three of these got into some sort of trouble for so doing. Other tragedies were suppressed for merely seeming to reflect too closely on contemporary affairs; one example is Daniel's *Philotas* (1605), which in some respects offered parallels to the fall of the Earl of Essex. Still other tragedies employed satirical carica-tures of living contemporaries in minor roles; the most notable example is Fletcher's *The Bloody Brother* (1617), which attacks the astrologers Bubb, Fiske and Bretnor by introducing corrupt and venal astrologers called De Bubie, La-Fiske, and Norbret into the play, and having them whipped and hanged in the fifth act. We know also of another tragedy or tragi-comedy that featured caricatures of people still living, namely the lost *Keep the Widow Waking* by Dekker, Rowley, Ford, and Webster, which was the subject of legal action in the summer of 1624, the same year as *A Game at Chess*. All these are excluded from a study where one of the main concerns—which one sees fought out in the personations of the War of the Theatres—is the nature of comedy as a genre. Furthermore, as indicated above, this study is concerned with establishing how per-sonation works when it is certainly present. Excluded for this reason are plays such as Shakespeare's *Love's Labour's Lost* or Lyly's court comedies,

15

where recent criticism has tended to doubt the existence of the personations that have at times been ascribed to them.

What is left falls into four main categories. Firstly, there are the plays of the War of the Theatres, in which Jonson on the one hand, and Marston and Dekker on the other, engage in quite sophisticated theoretical argument about the nature of professional comedy through the medium of stage caricatures of each other. Secondly, there are satirical comedies of the remainder of James's reign, of which this study considers four at length: *The Whore of Babylon*, *The Roaring Girl*, *Swetnam the Woman-hater*, and *A Game at Chess*. Thirdly, there are the plays of Jonson after the War of the Theatres, which continue to flirt with the possibilities of personation. Finally, the rivalries in the 1630s between dramatists that can broadly be labelled "courtly" and "professional" occasionally boil over into personation, most notably in Richard Brome's *The Court Begger* (1640); here too the personation coincides with and is part of struggles both theoretical and practical over the definition and control of professional drama—struggles that were still unresolved at the start of the Civil War. But first, it is necessary to outline the background evidence that satirical personation did indeed happen upon the English professional stage. It can be shown that personation, or at least the possibility of it, was a point of contention in criticism of the professional stage right from the earliest days of its establishment.

A good place to start is with the antitheatrical pamphlets of Stephen Gosson, humanist and renegade playwright. Gosson's primary objections to the stage relate to the sexual immorality of the theatre as an institution, but satirical drama too finds a place in his condemnation. In *Plays Confuted*, for instance, where Gosson is refuting the position that plays may offer moral education by displaying examples of vice to be avoided, he argues that such moral edification would require a "spirit of meeknes" in actors and poets which he doubts they possess. In particular,

> It appeareth by antiquitie, that the *Poets* which were before, had another meaning: for as any man had displeased them, to reuenge theire owne cause they studied to present him vpon the stage, there did they ruffle, and taunt; scoffe, and nippe; thunder, and lighten, and spue vp theire counning to deface him. Whereupon grewe one of the lawes of the twelue tables, that no man should be so hardie as to write any thing, whereby the good name of any bodie might be hurte.[7]

Poets, he claims, write against vice not out of sorrow or compassion, but out of

Mallice, for so *Eupolis* handled *Alcibiades*; or of corruption, as *Aristophanes* dealt with *Socrates* and *Cleon*; with *Socrates*, in his Comedie called *The cloudes*, wherin he was hyred by *Anytus* and *Melitus* to discredit him. . . .[8]

As becomes clear from the reference to Aristophanes, Gosson is referring in particular to Greek Old Comedy. Aristophanes, the only writer of Old Comedy whose plays survive in substantial quantities, was well known in the Renaissance, and not just for the incident alluded to by Gosson, when Socrates is said to have attended a performance of *Clouds* in which he himself was represented on stage. Numerous Greek editions and Latin translations attest to the appeal of Aristophanes in sixteenth-century Europe, and comparison between him and contemporary drama is a tactic frequently adopted by both attackers and defenders of the practice of personation.[9]

In fact, it was one adopted by Gosson's adversary Thomas Lodge, who, in replying to Gosson's pamphlets, argues that comedy's virtue lies precisely in the direct satire that it can offer. Indeed, his argument in favour of *ad hominem* satire is itself *ad hominem*, making particular reference to Gosson's own former career in the theatre:

> Whereupon Eupolis with Cratinus and Aristophanes began to write, and with ther eloquenter vaine and perfection of stil dyd more seuerely speak agaynst the abuses . . . which Horace himselfe witnesseth. For, sayth he, ther was no abuse but these men reprehended it; a thefe was loth to be seene [at] one [of] there spectacle[s], a coward was neuer present at theyr assemblies, a backbiter abhord that company; and I my selfe could not haue blamed you (Gosson) for exempting yourselfe from this theater; of troth I should have lykt your pollicy. . . . Yea, would God our realme could light vppon a Lucilius; then should the wicked bee poynted out from the good; a harlot woulde seeke no harbor at stage plais, lest she shold here her owne name growe in question. . . . As for you, I am sure of this one thing, he would paint you in your players ornaments. . . . And if we had some Satericall Poetes nowe a dayes to penn our commedies, that might be admitted of zeale to discypher the abuses of the worlde in the person of notorious offenders, I knowe we should wisely ryd our assemblyes of many of your brotherhod.[10]

In short, comedy that represented living contemporaries was a topic of controversy among the very first critics of the English professional stage. However, that is not to say that it was in fact taking place; certainly, Lodge implies that it isn't, although he would like it to be. As is shown below, numerous references at the end of the 1590s—twenty years after Gosson and Lodge were writing—tend to indicate that by then, satirical personation was an established part of the theatrical repertoire. Before that, however, information is harder to come by.

Critics have long argued over the comedies of Lyly, written in the 1580s. Some have read them as elaborate allegorical representations of prominent court figures, as personating in an oblique, almost Spenserian mode, while others—including most recent writers—have argued that such allegorical readings are fanciful and misguided. As stated above, this study is concerned with establishing the mechanics of personation where it is known to have happened, so Lyly's comedies are set aside here, as are the allegations concerning *Love's Labour's Lost*.[11]

Lyly himself was one of those involved in the anti-Marprelate plays of the end of the 1580s. Although these plays are lost, it is known that they flouted the pamphleteer Martin Marprelate, depicting him as a half-man, half-beast, and staging his ignominious death. They attracted comparison, both favourable and unfavourable, to the Greek Old Comedy, a touchstone for both Gosson and Lodge ten years earlier. Nonetheless, they cannot be considered as true personating comedy, for one very good reason: Martin Marprelate himself did not exist, but was merely a *nom de plume* for an unknown polemicist. The plays written against him appear to have been sponsored by the bishops, a situation which gives rise to several paradoxes. Indeed, one could argue that being actualised in performance in these plays, and given a real body to be killed in, gave Marprelate the solidity to catch the public imagination, and went a long way towards defining what one contemporary observer called "Martinomania." Secondly, it is a critical commonplace that the encouragement given by the bishops to anti-Marprelate pamphleteers such as Thomas Nashe was a contributing factor in the rise of the intemperate, polemical prose style that Nashe, for instance, later went on to use with such effect against Gabriel Harvey. Likewise, I suggest, an important precedent for libellous personation on the English stage was set by the Marprelate plays, again through the agency of the bishops.[12]

All the same, one still looks in vain for direct evidence that representation of living people took place upon the professional stage, until a cluster of references to the practice right at the very turn of the century, in the years which have been identified, by different critics and for different reasons, as marking a watershed in the development of the professional theatre. For instance, it is a long-standing contention that the bishops' ban on verse satire of 1599, in response to the form's growing frankness of satirical attack, and including within its terms the prose works of Thomas Nashe, meant that the evident public appetite for such satire had to be satisfied in other markets.[13] Another argument is offered by Jonathan Haynes, who suggests that a major change is the arrival of city comedy set in London, as opposed to Florence or Rome. The shift is marked by plays like Haughton's *Englishmen for my Money* (1598) or Chapman's *An Humorous Day's Mirth* (1597), which also claims the distinction of being one of the first plays to use the concept of "humours."[14] Haynes further links both these phenomena to the change that replaced "playing" with "personation" as a new buzz word for the activities of actors. Meanwhile, Richard Helgerson, working from a completely different angle, has also identified 1599 as a pivotal year in the development of English drama: the year that Robert Armin replaced William Kemp as chief clown in Shakespeare's company, and the year that the company moved to the newly-opened Globe Theatre. He suggests that both these events are symptomatic of "the alienation of the clown from the playwright, of the players' theater from the authors' theater, of the people from the nation and its canonical self-representations."[15]

From this same period one starts to find evidence for the practice of personation of living people. For instance, Rowland Whyte wrote to Robert Sidney on 26 October 1599 that he had seen a stage representation of the siege of Turnholt, in which the actors imitated the appearance of individual noblemen:

> And all your Names vsed that were at yt; especially *Sir Fra. Veres,* and he that plaid that Part gott a Beard resembling his and a Watchett Sattin Doublett, with Hose trimd with Siluer Lace. You was also introduced, Killing, Slaying, and Overthrowing the *Spaniards.*[16]

This play, describing events of 1598 a year after they happen and representing living people under their real names, is lost. There is no reason to suppose that this representation was satirical; rather, it seems to have been a patriotic celebration, perhaps a distant forerunner of something like Dekker's *Whore of Babylon* (although, as will later be shown, that play—in spite of its patriotic mode—has many points of contact with satirical comedy).

There is a revealing outburst from the Earl of Essex, in a letter of 12 May 1600, who after complaining about libels against him of various sorts concludes, "Shortly they shall play me in what forms they list upon the stage."[17] Almost exactly a year later, a Privy Council Order for 10 May 1601 asked the Middlesex justices to investigate a play at the Curtain in which were depicted the persons of some gentlemen of good desert and quality that are yet alive, under obscure manner, but yet in such sort as all the hearers may take notice both of the matter and of the persons that are meant thereby.[18]

This play, yet again, is lost.

Also in 1601 come the three Whipper Pamphlets, starting with the anonymous *The Whipping of the Satyre*. These doggerel verses, attacking one another for railing of various sorts, have like the War of the Theatres afforded much ammunition to critics interested in biographical speculation. But what is of interest for the matter at hand is that one of the people attacked is a "Humorist" who to some extent at least is a caricature of Ben Jonson and whose crime consists of a tendency to "Mocke, deride, mis-call, / Reuile, scoffe, flout, defame and slaunder" living people in stage comedies.[19]

All this is anecdotal. One has no impartial yardstick to measure a change in the frequency of representations of real people on the Renaissance stage. But since anecdotes are all we have, it is striking how the ones recorded do cluster in the years around the turn of the century, as if they were marking a definite shift in climate: towards a more ambitious, author-driven theatre, more prepared to represent realistic things and possibly even from time to time real people. And it is in this context—of dynamic changes within the world of professional drama—that one must see the notorious and much-maligned "War of the Theatres."

CHAPTER ONE

Jonson and the War of the Theatres

First of all, a note on terms. The different names of the War of the Theatres reflect different conceptions of what it might be: the choice is between the old term "Stage-Quarrel," which portrays the conflict as a personal feud between dramatists; "The War of the Theatres," favoured by most critics, which sees it as an argument between the different dramatic companies; or "The Poetomachia" or Poets' War, favoured by some more recent writers, in which it is viewed as an argument between poets and about poetry. The third of these has the best contemporary warrant, being Dekker's own term for the quarrel.[1] Unluckily, it's a deliberately hideous word, a parodically pedantic coinage. In this study, therefore, the more conventional term "War of the Theatres" is preferred.

The indisputable, or at any rate least disputable, part of the War of the Theatres centres upon *Poetaster* and *Satiromastix*. In *Poetaster* Jonson is attacking personally enemies of his. He claims as much, or rather his simulacrum "The Author" does, in the "Apologetical Dialogue" affixed to the work. It is also undoubted that *Satiromastix*, by Thomas Dekker, is related to *Poetaster*—a play which it names several times in its preface—and constitutes an attack on Jonson in the person of Horace. Thus far there is no disagreement.[2]

Beyond this, the boundaries are unclear, and there is a monograph to be written on the history of criticism of the War of the Theatres, which would form a good appendix to Schoenbaum's *Shakespeare's Lives*. Serious interest in the "War" first developed when critics starving for biographical information about Shakespeare started to ransack the plays of Jonson in search of references to him and caricatures of him. Needless to say, much promising material was found, and William Gifford in his landmark 1816 edition of Jonson was forced to spend a lot of time repudiating a currently held belief that Jonson's plays were mainly exercises in maligning his rival.[3] And once Shakespeare scholars had set the precedent, the second half of the nineteenth century saw criticism of plays relating to the War spiral into an elaborate system of tables of identifications.

This material, which went out of fashion along with the biographical criticism that created it, is no longer credited. The well-known study by R. A. Small put paid to most of the identifications that had been made, while subsequent work by Herford and Simpson and by O. J. Campbell further defined the limits of the quarrel.[4] But from the 1930s until very recently, little critical attention has been paid to the War *per se.* In fact, in their eagerness to distance themselves from discredited critical practices, critics have gone to the other extreme and have tended to deny that the War ever happened. Work on Marston, whose reputation was felt to be especially damaged by viewing him just as a foil to Jonson, shows this tendency most strongly. In 1969 Philip Finkelpearl offered new interpretations of *Jack Drum's Entertainment* and *What You Will* which deny that they relate to Ben Jonson or the War, interpretations followed by many subsequent writers on Marston.[5] As for Dekker, Cyrus Hoy's notes on Fredson Bowers' edition of Dekker deal well and sensibly with the War as it pertains to *Satiromastix,* but much other recent work —notably Julia Gasper's study of Dekker's "Militant Protestantism"— avoids the War as far as possible.[6]

In the last ten years, however, there has been an upsurge of interest in the War, read for various broadly biographical purposes. David Mann uses it as a quarry for information about the social history of actors; Jonathan Haynes as a basis for a reading of these plays in terms of both commercial and cultural economics; and James Bednarz and James Shapiro both revive the idea of Shakespeare's involvement as participant and victim, on the basis of echoes and parallel passages.[7] But the fact remains that as a phenomenon the War of the Theatres is almost unique in Renaissance English drama. It is the only case where the victims of stage satire respond in kind, with plays of their own, which challenge the assumptions of their rivals' plays. The War therefore represents a dialogue about the nature and assumptions of drama which is a lot more valuable than any biographical facts to be gleaned from it.[8]

The chronology established by Small was taken over by O. J. Campbell, Herford and Simpson, and Cyrus Hoy with only slight developments and disagreements, and has been most recently endorsed and refined by Tom Cain in his edition of *Poetaster.*[9] It will be convenient to repeat it here.

At some point in 1599, it would appear that John Marston had a hand in writing *Histriomastix* (published 1610), a strange and unwieldy six-act play about the relationship between prosperity and society.[10] Jonson appears to have taken the character of Chrisoganus the scholar, perhaps intended as a compliment, as in some respect a personal slight. When Jonson wrote *Every Man Out of his Humour* later in 1599 (published 1600) he included two characters, Clove and Orange, "Meere strangers to the whole scope of our play" (III.i.18-19) who spoke fustian —meaningless pretentious vocabulary of the sort affected by Marston, and including incidentally some of the words given to Chrisoganus by Marston. It is possible that these characters never appeared on stage, but were among the extra unacted material Jonson claims to have introduced in the printed version: but the effect was the same.

Dekker, Marston (probably) and Jonson had collaborated on a tragedy with a Scottish theme in September 1599, implying reasonably amicable relations between them, but in 1600 Marston's *Jack Drum's Entertainment* was produced. Brabant Senior is generally, although not universally, regarded as a caricature of Jonson. In the autumn of that year, with a probable court performance at Christmas, Jonson followed with *Cynthia's Revels* (published 1601), in which Hedon and Anaides are taken to represent Marston and Dekker.

Marston's *What You Will* (April 1601, suggests Small, although the play's most recent editor is reluctant to be so specific), published 1607, satirises Jonson in the character of Lampatho Doria. Jonson's *Poetaster* (published 1602) personates Marston and Dekker as Crispinus and Demetrius, and furthermore makes personal and specific insults against the players they are involved with, who are, however, not represented on the stage. Thomas Dekker makes his intervention in the quarrel with *Satiromastix* (published 1602), an attack on Jonson in the person of Horace, and after that no more is heard. Traditional dating assigned *Poetaster* and *Satiromastix* to June and August of 1601 respectively, but recently Tom Cain has argued persuasively that both plays were staged in the winter at the end of 1601. At any rate, no more plays were written specifically addressing the feud after this point.[11]

Thus in this version of events three plays by Jonson are implicated in the War—*Every Man Out*, *Cynthia's Revels*, and *Poetaster*. His opponents contribute four—*Histriomastix, Jack Drum's Entertainment, What You Will*, and *Satiromastix*. In the earlier plays, the personation is more tenuous and less central to the concerns of the play; but as the War goes on, the personations become more extensive, bitter, and biographically specific. The plays become more explicit in their satirical intent and more ingenious in their defences of it.

This can be seen in Jonson's three plays. *Every Man Out of his Humour* includes one scene satirising Marstonian vocabulary, irrelevant to the main plot. *Cynthia's Revels* introduces characters whose satirical reference is made moderately clear, and defends this personation implicitly. Finally, *Poetaster* is explicit about its purpose and very circumstantial in its portraits.

Likewise, on the other side, Chrisoganus in *Histriomastix* is so shadowy we can hardly tell whether the character is intended as serious or risible, let alone how it might relate to Jonson. *Jack Drum's Entertainment* is a messy, miscellaneous play which happens to include among one of its numerous elements a character with a discernible resemblance to Jonson. But analysis of *What You Will* and *Satiromastix* will reveal that these plays, in the same pattern as the Jonson plays, become more explicit in their poetics and in their personation. Marston and Dekker are discussed in the next chapter, but for now it remains to show how Ben Jonson's early comical satires develop the idea of satirical drama as a literary phenomenon and use representation of living people as one of the techniques to argue this point.

Every Man Out

It is a familiar contention that Jonson is eager to stress the literariness of his work as a marker of how it is uniquely different from his rivals'—as Suckling quipped, "His were call'd Works, where others were but Plaies."[12] Jonson's 1616 Folio, for instance, is widely recognised as just such an endeavour, and a continuation of the classicising tendency of the printing conventions of his early quartos.[13] In the case of *Every Man Out*, the same assertion of literary merit is acheived by means of the "framing" characters—Mitis, Cordatus, and Asper. What they offer, in fact, is a stage equivalent of a marginal gloss, such as might be found in Renaissance editions of Terence: an assertion of literary affinity made especially pointed by the fact that two of them—Cordatus and Asper—bear the names of prominent commentators upon the Latin comedian.[14]

MITIS: How is't?

CORDATUS: Faith sir, I must refraine to iudge, only this I can say of it, 'tis strange, and of a particular kind by it selfe, somewhat like *Vetus Comoedia*: a worke that hath bounteously pleased me, how it will answere the generall expectation, I know not.

MITIS: Does he obserue all the lawes of *Comedie* in it?

CORDATUS: What lawes meane you?

MITIS: Why, the equall diuision of it into *Acts*, and *Scenes*, according to the *Terentian* manner, his true number of Actors; the furnishing of the *Scene*

with GREX, or CHORUS, and that the whole Argument fall within com-
passe of a dayes businesse.

CORDATUS: O no, these are too nice obseruations. (Induction 229-42)

Cordatus then goes on to give an account of the genesis of comedy,
following in most important respects Donatus, with circumstantial details derived from "some Renaissance critic":[15]

> 'Tis extant, that that which we call *Comoedia*, was at first nothing but a simple,
> and continued *Song*, sung by one only person, till SUSARIO inuented a
> second, after him EPICHARMUS a third; PHORMUS, and CHIONIDES de-
> uised to haue foure Actors, with a *Prologue* and *Chorus*; to which CRATINUS
> (long after) added a fift, and sixt; EUPOLIS more; ARISTOPHANES more
> then they: euery man in the dignitie of his spirit and iudgement, supplyed
> something. And (though that in him this kinde of *Poeme* appeared absolute,
> and fully perfected) yet how is the face of it chang'd since. . . .
>
> (Induction 250-61)

Cordatus insists, you will notice, that comedy is a "kinde of *Poeme*,"
part of an evolving literary tradition founded upon classical models. As
will be seen, many of Jonson's colleagues and rivals did not share this
essentially literary paradigm of professional drama, and in the course of
the War of the Theatres they argue cogently and elegantly against it. So
on this count alone the assertions of Cordatus are provocative.

More surprising is the fact that direct personal satire is also made
central to the agenda of the play here. A particular sort of comedy that is
dwelt upon is what Cordatus calls *Vetus Comoedia*—Greek Old Comedy,
as in the works of Aristophanes. And what Old Comedy was most famous
for, as seen above with reference to Gosson and Lodge, was the representation on stage of living people.

When it comes to scholarship on the reception of Aristophanes,
Northrop Frye has a lot to answer for. His structuralist terminology of
"Old Comedy" and "New Comedy" as archetypical, almost mythological
forms based on certain character types has led a generation of critics to
assume that this is how Greek Old Comedy has always been regarded.
But this is not true. Old Comedy, to Renaissance critics, was remarkable overwhelmingly for its personal satire.[16] As for Aristophanes' col-
league Eupolis, mentioned by Cordatus, Francis Meres compared him
to Thomas Nashe for the frankness and personal specificity of his satire:
"As Eupolis of Athens vsed great libertie in taxing the vices of men: so
doth Thomas Nash, witness the broode of the Harueys!"[17] In other
words, the model of satire mentioned in Jonson's Induction is at once

unusually literary—in its reference to recondite Greek authors—*and* unusually topical: these two modes, usually perceived as opposites, are brought together by Jonson's choice of literary exemplar.

Furthermore, the idea that the play might contain dangerously frank, dangerously personal satire is reiterated by Jonson's characters themselves. Asper, for one, insists that there is personal representation going on, scorning the danger in which this puts him from men "growne impatient of reproofe":

> If any, here, chance to behold himselfe,
> Let him not dare to challenge me of wrong,
> For, if he shame to haue his follies knowne,
> First he should shame to act 'hem.
> (Prologue 140-43)

And he asks Mitis and Cordatus to look out for "a gallant of this marke" in the audience, with crossed arms, hat pulled down low, who will offer a running commentary on the play. Asper is particularly on the look-out for such people, with a view to giving them "pills to purge": namely, by making them the objects of his satire, a satire which takes dramatic form. At another point, Mitis and Cordatus allude to the possibility of personal satire even while denying that it is taking place, making a digression to inform any "narrow-ey'd decypherers" in the audience that "the author defies them" (Induction 175; II.vi.171-75).

Again, it is surprising how an eagerness to be topical and specific is justified in terms of established literary values, and presented as a highbrow alternative to conventional fare. For instance, Mitis comments on the sort of action to be expected in an ordinary play: "as of a duke to be in loue with a countesse, and that countesse to bee in loue with the dukes sonne, and the sonne to loue the ladies waiting maid: some such crosse wooing, with a clowne to their seruingman, better then to be thus neere, and familiarly allied to the time." But Cordatus' response is to quote Cicero, or at least Cicero as transmitted by Donatus and Minturno: comedy offers an "Imitatio vitae, Speculum consuetudinis, Imago veritatis" (an imitation of life, a mirror of custom, and an image of truth).[18]

On the one hand, the play suggested by Mitis appears to belong to the genre of romance most effectively criticised by Philip Sidney in terms that, as has often been remarked, are being echoed here; on the other hand, Cordatus praises as an antithesis of it something topical, referential, satirical, and quite different from the neo-classically stylised alternatives Sidney was envisaging. This technique of denigrating lesser comedy in order to justify satirical comedy in a Jonsonian mode will crop up again in *Poetaster*, organised around the image of the Tiber. While appearing to be aligning himself with Elizabethan critical orthodoxy, Jonson is in fact developing something new.

Jonson's reinterpretation of Donatus challenges previous interpretations by suggesting a different reading of the metaphors of reproduction: an imitation, a mirror, and an image, read not as indications of difference and distinction but as an argument for similarity. And Cordatus' use of Donatus' formula here as an apology for personally satirical comedy may be compared to Hamlet's use of it two years later as a justification for a far more transgressive cocktail of topical reference and personation at the Danish court.[19]

And yet, a modern critic attempting to locate personations in the play may well wonder where to start. Critical attention, such as there has been, has centred upon five characters: Clove, Orange, Shift, Carlo Buffone, and the Queen who appears at the end. The first of these may be dealt with quickly. Judging from echoes of Marston's works, it seems likely that the "fustian" that Clove and Orange spout during their brief appearance in the play serves as a satire of Marstonian vocabulary.[20] On the other hand, these characters have no role in the plot, and they don't act like the personations of Marston that Jonson certainly does create later, so one can't say that they're representations or personations of Marston.

Next to be considered are Captain Shift and Carlo Buffone, who are named by Jasper Mayne in a poem in *Jonsonus Virbius* among those characters whom Jonson was accused of having taken from life.[21] (Mayne, indeed, describes such personation with reference specifically to Aristophanes.) With Shift, a spirited attempt has been made by E. A. G. Honigmann to identify him with John Weever, whom Honigmann also proposes as a model for *What You Will*'s Simplicius and *Satiromastix*' Asinius Bubo.[22] Hongimann's argument is ingenious and deserves more serious discussion than it will get here, but it is hampered by a lack of contemporary attestation beyond disputable verbal echoes, which means that methodologically it remains at the level of very plausible guesswork and as such outside the strict scope of this study.

As for Carlo Buffone, John Aubrey goes further even than Mayne, independently reporting gossip that named the alleged original—a braggart named Charles Chester, prominent in tavern society in the 1590s. Aubrey's allegation finds reinforcement in other satire against Chester by writers including Nashe, Harington, Dekker, and Guilpin.

The previous critical consensus has been to give a grudging acceptance to this identification and then to forget about it, since the issue of tavern-railers such as Chester has not been seen as central to the War of the Theatres or comical satire. But given that Carlo is one of the lynchpins of the play, this identification should not be passed over so lightly. I argue elsewhere that it is a mistake to overlook the satire against Chester, and that a large part of *Every Man Out* is devoted to denigrating the oral satire offered by Carlo/Chester as part of a project of developing an oppositional definition of "comical satire" as something literary, morally justifiable, and worthwhile. The argument is too lengthy to enter into here, but the case of Carlo Buffone shows at the very least that *Every Man Out* was a play which among its early audiences and readers invited personally satirical "decipherment."[23] In any case, all these examples—Clove, Orange, Shift, and Carlo—seem almost insignificant before the fifth and final possible example of personation in this play. In its original form *Every Man Out of his Humour* did put one character on stage that represented a living person: namely, Queen Elizabeth.

The representation of Elizabeth, whose mere appearance is sufficient to jolt Macilente out of his humour seems to have been too controversial and to have been suppressed. Jonson included the original ending in the quarto printing of the play, explaining that he had had to withdraw it "Διὰ τὸ τὴν Βασίλισσαν προσωποποιεῖσθαι" ("Because of the personation of the Queen").[24] The Greek phrase flaunts both the learnedness of the device, and more specifically, its precedents in Greek Old Comedy. For instance, the Queen of Heaven whose unexpected appearance at the climax of Aristophanes' *Birds* is the reward of Peisthetaerus, is a βασίλεα (βασίλισσα is a slightly rarer variant of this word). Helen Ostovich has persuasively argued that this scene from *Birds* may be a model for Jonson's ending, in that both feature a change of register within a satirical comedy, and an arrival of a queen at the last moment. She has also pointed out that προσωποποιεῖσθαι is a metaphor from Old Comedy, referring to the masks that were used in performance of it.[25] Jonson is once again, as in the Induction, using Aristophanes as a precedent that justifies his own representation of living people, even though in the case of this final incident the representation is celebratory rather than satirical.

So, an important element of *Every Man Out*, even perhaps its thematic centre, is its representation of living people. Jonson links this representation with literary traditions, notably Greek Old Comedy, as a way of asserting a new type of comic drama. In Jonson's next play, *Cynthia's*

28

Revels, not merely does the same sort of representation take place, but even the act of representation is itself represented on stage.

Cynthia's Revels

Cynthia's Revels has been given a hard time by Jonson criticism. Its fate is to be mentioned rather than discussed, to be glossed over as quickly as possible, while most writers, indeed, concur explicitly or implicitly with the verdict of Jonas Barish, who called it "a great fossilized dinosaur of a play."[26] The worst problem, for many, is the dearth of plot in any conventional sense: nothing really happens for most of the course of the play, as the gallants are simply playing games to kill time. But again, I suggest, a key element in this play is the representation of living contemporaries, used as part of a programme to redefine the status of comic drama. In this light, *Cynthia's Revels* regains an urgency that most modern critics find sadly lacking in it.

But first of all, why suspect that there is any personal reference at all in this play? The best external evidence is to be found in Dekker's *Satiromastix*, in which lines from this play are put into the mouth of "Horace," an acknowledged representation of Jonson under the name of one of his own characters from *Poetaster*. In *Satiromastix* these lines from *Cynthia's Revels* are applied, not as originally to Hedon and Anaides, but to Dekker's sympathetic characters Crispinus and Demetrius, who certainly do represent Marston and Dekker. So Dekker, at least, conflates Hedon and Anaides with Crispinus and Demetrius, seeing both pairs as representations of himself and John Marston. Furthermore, passages from *Cynthia's Revels* appear, modified and subverted, in Marston's *What You Will*, which also appears to be a personally satirical answer to this play. Given these two examples of contemporary interpretation, it seems reasonable to accept—for the moment—that there is some sort of personal reference going on, focussed upon Hedon and Anaides.

Hedon and Anaides are two gallants with a literary bent, generic representatives of unwisdom rather than detailed depictions of Elizabethan playwrights; they can't be called portraits of Marston and Dekker, or at best, only very stylised ones.[27] Their faults are self-love, envy, and frivolity, and their punishment by the exemplary Crites takes a most unusual form, that of mockery by impersonation:

> I will play all his owne play before him; court the wench, in his garbe, in his phrase, with his face; leaue him not so much as a looke, an eye, a stalke, or an imperfect oth, to expresse himselfe by, after me. (V.iv.571-74)

29

Crites fulfils this threat, mimicking Hedon and Anaides to their faces with such devastating satirical effect that neither of them speaks again within the play. So his remark about depriving them of the means to express themselves is no empty hyperbole. Interestingly, this seizure of an enemy's ability to speak is a repeated theme in the climaxes of Jonson's comical satires. In *Every Man Out*, it is Carlo Buffone whose mouth is sealed with molten wax. In *Poetaster*, the luckless Crispinus is the victim of a medical purgation that makes him literally vomit up his vocabulary. In both cases, these silencings are directed at thinly disguised representations of Jonson's contemporaries. *Poetaster's* Crispinus certainly is an attack upon John Marston: and, as mentioned above, Carlo Buffone has generally been identified as the notorious railer Charles Chester.

If we examine *Cynthia's Revels* with this pattern in mind, the focus of the play, towards which all the preceding action is geared, is not so much the final masques as Crites' cataclysmic impersonation of Hedon and Anaides, a synecdoche for Jonson's personation of Marston and Dekker. The play is designed to engineer an imaginative situation in which such an overtly aggressive action becomes sympathetic, legitimate and laudable. This programme is already under way in the Induction, even before the action proper begins.

The Induction starts to establish a dichotomy between two strands of imagery about drama: one which presents it in terms of its literariness and its moral function, and one which demonises it according to these standards. Of course, the play *Cynthia's Revels* is presented in the imagery of the former type: "The title of his play is CYNTHIAS *Reuels*, as any man (that hath hope to bee saued by his booke) can witnesse" (Induction 39-40), we are told, with a deftly flippant reference to the custom of benefit of clergy whereby a literate man could avoid the gallows once, a custom to which Jonson had had recourse only the previous year after his killing of Gabriel Spencer.[28] While literally referring to the "title" written on a board above the stage, Jonson takes an opportunity to establish the idea of the whole play as a text needing to be read—not just a mere performance. On the other hand, plays by others are subjected to criticisms which rehearse some standard points:

> It is in the generall behalf eof this fair societie here, that I am to speake, at least the more iudicious part of it, which seemes much distasted with the immodest and obscene writing of manie, in their playes. Besides, they could wish, your *Poets* would leaue to bee promoters of other mens iests, and to way-lay all the stale *apothegmes*, or olde bookes, they can heare of (in print, or otherwise) to farce their *Scenes* withall. That they would not so penuriously

gleane wit, from euerie laundresse, or hackney-man, or deriue their best
grace (with seruile imitation) from common stages, or obseruation of the
companie they conuerse with.   (Induction 173-83)

It is not new to revile the obscenity of plays. The distaste for "observation" and realism in comedy is something which fits with the insistence
of Sidney *et al.* that comedy is stylised, fictive and unreal, although
normally they like to think of it as conventional in subject-matter as well.
Jonson twists the dislike of realism into a dislike of convention: whereas
Jonson is normally a strong advocate of precedent, here he opposes it.
It's interesting to compare this to *Every Man Out* where a dislike of
hackneyed inferior drama is made into an argument *in favour of* comedy
"neere, and familiarly allied to the time." Jonson's poetics are a flexible,
polemical tool.

The dramatic paradigms brought up in the Induction are meant to
condition responses, not just to the play *Cynthia's Revels*, but to the
various plays within that play. *Cynthia's Revels* rests upon the conceit that
some of its characters, notably Amorphus, Asotus, Hedon and Anaides,
are living their lives as bad plays. In other words, this declaration of
originality here is partly as one would expect a comment on *Cynthia's
Revels*, but mainly a comment on the plays that we will see being lived out
by the four gallants.

In Act II, for instance, Hedon and Anaides (themselves would-be
masque-writers) are seen attempting to rehearse a series of witticisms to
"act" wherewith to impress their fellow-courtiers—a dramatic strategy
that, we later learn, fails when Crites accidentally interrupts the execu-
tion of it. Amorphus later reassures Asotus, who is equally nervous about
his court performance as a "*neophyte*-player," and describes the incident
in the following terms: "There was HEDON, and ANAIDES, (farre more
practis'd gallants then your selfe) who were both out, to comfort you"
(II.ii.73; III.i.3, 5-7). "Out," as a technical term for a player who has
forgotten his lines, serves to make explicit the connection between
courtly role-playing and theatre. Trying to think of ways to avoid the
same situation occurring again, Amorphus suggests that one of Asotus'
problems is lack of material, and offers a solution:

AMORPHUS: As your eares do meet with a new *phrase*, or an acute jest, take it
in: a quicke nimble memory will lift it away, and at your next publique
meale, it is your owne.

ASOTUS: But I shall neuer vtter it perfectly, sir.   (III.i.42-46)

31

This sort of plagiarism is precisely the method for acquiring new material that is condemned in the Induction in connection with playwrights. Again, bad writing and bad personal manners are linked together. Play imagery continues a few scenes later when Crites too muses on the resemblance between Cynthia's court and stage drama:

> There stands a *Neophyte* glazing of his face,
> Pruning his clothes, perfuming of his haire,
> Against his idoll enters; and repeates
> (Like an vnperfect *prologue*, at third musike)
> His part of speeches, and confederate iests,
> In passion to himselfe. Another sweares
> His *Scene* of courtship ouer . . .
> . . . .
> A fourth, he onely comes in for a *mute*:
> Diuides the *act* with a dumbe shew, and *exit*.
> Then must the ladies laugh, straight comes their *Scene*,
> A sixt times worse confusion then the rest.
>
> (III.iv.55-61, 71-74)

This is specific, too, about what sort of drama is being acted out in the court: a comedy that includes that morally suspect commodity, laughter. And it is not merely that the courtiers behave like characters on a stage; in the case of the gallant who swears "his *Scene* of courtship ouer," the court is self-consciously borrowing the language of the drama. Drama pervades their behaviour and how they think about their behaviour. Drama also *is* their behaviour. There are several plays-within-plays contemplated or executed in *Cynthia's Revels*, including the gallants' projected masque and the two masques finally performed. There are other ludic uses of language such as word-games and love-songs.[29] This may seem like the sort of involuted self-referentiality proposed by Jackson Cope as typical of Renaissance thinking about stage fictions, but actually it is part of a satirical attack against the self-indulgence of those who think of their own lives in this way. As Robert N. Watson has observed, "Metadrama, which serves to blur the distinction between art and life in so many Renaissance plays, serves in Jonsonian comedy to insist upon that distinction."[30]

The gallants are not very good at invention, and they flesh their self-written parts out with "play-particles" and material from books; furthermore, they steal material from others, as seen above. As well as living their lives as plays, the gallants also attempt to write plays. The *ad hominem* twist in this—that Hedon and Anaides represent two actual playwrights—has the special effect of burying these two characters in multiple levels of fiction, reducing them and their fictitious colleagues Amorphus and Asotus to the level of "puppets."[31] The fictive unreality of it all is emphasiszed by the "deciphering" of these characters by Mercury disguised as a page. The fact that he can offer such succinct definitions of them, reading them as if they were a code, suggests that like the characters of comedy described by Sidney as possessing a "signifying badge," they are stereotypical and incapable of real development or change.[32]

In this connection Anaides' squire is an especially complicating figure. Anaides

> lightly occupies the iesters roome at the table, and keepes *laughter*, GELAIA (a wench in pages attire) following him in place of a squire, whom he now and then tickles with some strange ridiculous stuffe. (II.ii.81-5)

Gelaia is a cipher, a characterless abstraction; she is a concrete form of the worst nightmares of an anti-stage writer such as Stephen Gosson, for whom laughter was a morally reprehensible activity that in making a man lose voluntary control of his body would "effeminate" him.[33] Furthermore, she herself cross-dresses, confusing enough in a theatre where all the performers are male anyway, and especially since this transvestite custom was a major plank of the attack against them. Not merely does the reference to tickling confirm this view of laughter (after all, Sidney called it a "scornful tickling"), but it reinforces the idea of her sexual relationship with Anaides. As a motivation for transvestitism it echoes on one level the Rosalinds and Violas of romantic comedy, but debased into the disguise of a mere "punquetto": revealing the immorality which to the antitheatrical mind lay concealed not far beneath the specious surface of these dramas, and recalling the allegations that theatres provided many opportunities for such women to ply their trade.[34]

Anaides' reliance on Gelaia is a metaphor for Dekker's dramatic style, and for his private manners; Jonson's concern is to link the two. As well as being represented in Gelaia, laughter reappears several times in the play as a motif. Hedon's attempt to use laughter to hurt and humiliate (III.ii.10) is contrasted with the true corrective use of laughter in satire as praised by Sidney: to "make a man laugh at folly, and at length ashamed, to laugh at himself, which he cannot avoid without avoiding the folly."[35] In *Cynthia's Revels* the stratagem of Mercury and Crites, developed in Act V, shows this ideal in action. As Mercury says:

It is our purpose, CRITES, to correct,
And punish, with our laughter, this nights sport
Which our court-*Dors* so heartily intend:
And by that worthy scorne, to make them know
How farre beneath the dignitie of man
Their serious, and most practis'd actions are.

(V.i.17-22)

Crites' personation of Hedon and Anaides is justified, since the thrust of
the play is to prove that they are already personating themselves—that
their lives are nothing real, but a tissue of fictions. These fictions of the
gallants are associated with the very worst of contemporary drama,
especially as represented by Gelaia, and opposed to the morally improving drama of Crites in his masque and on the wider level to *Cynthia's
Revels* itself. In normal circumstances, reasons Jonson, comedy should
function by sparing the persons and taxing the crimes, but this is not
possible because the crime is precisely the creation of such a "person" as
the public facade of Hedon.

When the gallants see themselves mimicked by Crites, and the veil of
self-conceit drawn, the effect is impressive. Mercury tells the horrified
Anaides he is "cossen'd of [his] courtship" (V.iv.591-92). Anaides says
nothing in reply, indeed, never speaks again. He has indeed been
deprived of everything, and as Crites forecast does not retain even "an
imperfect oth, to expresse himselfe by." Meanwhile, Crites in his personation of Hedon links the plagiarism of the gallants to the falsely
praised beauty of their escorts: "You that tell your Mistris, Her beautie is
all composde of theft; Her haire stole from APOLLO'S goldy-locks; Her
white and red, lillies, and roses stolne out of paradise" (V.iv.598-600).
Crites' personation is both a plagiarism and an exposure of plagiarism:
he steals Anaides' courtship and Hedon's metaphors, but the courtship
and the metaphors did not belong to them in the first place. *Cynthia's
Revels* is constructed around showing that this action—and hence the
play *Cynthia's Revels* itself, for which Crites' mimicry acts as a sort of
synecdoche—was justified.

Echo and imitation are appropriate themes for a play which opens
with an appearance from Echo herself. The fountain of self-love that she
creates with her curse is pointedly contrasted with Helicon early in the
play. And after all the delusive reflections of the masques, the gallants
are despatched in search of Helicon, looking for good personal behaviour and good art at once. For such a play, where art and personal
morality are intertwined, the line "I will play all his owne play before
him" would serve well as an epigraph.

Poetaster

Cynthia's Revels, like *Every Man Out*, represents living people on stage as part of a concern to define good drama as against bad drama. This argument, applied to *Poetaster*, suddenly looks more familiar: it has long been recognised that this play is predicated upon the representation of living people, and that the question of the status of poetry is a central preoccupation of the play. In this analysis, I want to go further, and point out that in the paratexts of the play Jonson makes a link between what he calls "salt"—that is, frankness of satirical intent, shading into personation of individuals—and literary pedigree, a link which one has already seen made in *Every Man Out*. Again, as in *Every Man Out*, Old Comedy is one of the means through which this connection is made, invoked by Jonson's creation The Author in the Apologetical Dialogue, who defends his work against his fictional interlocutor Polyposus:

> POLYPOSUS: O, but they lay particular imputations—
>
> AUTHOR: As what?
>
> POLYPOSUS: That all your writing, is meere rayling.
>
> AUTHOR: Ha! If all the salt in the old *comoedy*
> Should be so censur'd, or the sharper wit
> Of the bold *satyre*, termed scolding rage,
> What age could then compare with those, for buffons?
> What should be sayd of ARISTOPHANES?
> PERSIUS? or IUVENAL? whose names we now
> So glorifie in schooles, at least pretend it.
> (Apologetical Dialogue 184-92)

In short, *Poetaster* is an Aristophanic satire, aimed against real people (which is, as we have seen, the distinguishing element of Aristophanic satire to the Renaissance), and set in a "Rome" of obvious contemporary relevance. The contemporaries in question, Dekker and Marston, are to be satirised as seedy poet-playwrights, immoral and, what's worse, inept. Envy, whose soliloquy begins the play, is (as Richard Dutton points out) unfortunately and inexplicably unable to see the contemporary reference that the Author intends:

> ROME? ROME? O my vext soule,
> How might I force this to the present state?
> Are there no players here? no poet-apes,
> That come with basiliskes eyes, whose forked tongues
> Are steept in venome, as their hearts in gall?[36]

As in *Cynthia's Revels*, the two different sets of imagery to describe things theatrical are developed early on. Envy's anticipation of "spie-like suggestions, priuie whisperings" picks up on fears of personal satire and concealed meanings.[37] The people who will help Envy think up these whisperings are the "players" and the "poet-Apes," with the players here imagined sitting in the audience as if on holiday, as if this play were a self-performing script not requiring their services at all. "Poet-Ape" is a direct quotation from Sidney's *Defence*.[38] And the connection between "poet-Apes" and "players" further recalls Sidney's "naughty play-makers and stage-keepers" in the way the association denies the author of stage-plays to be a proper writer.

On the other hand, what Envy is attacking is figured as a piece of text. She attempts to come up with an alternative reading of it "with sense-lesse glosses, and allusions," and wishes her allies to apply their venom:

> Helpe me to damne the Authour. Spit it foorth
> Vpon his lines, and shew your rustie teeth
> At euerie word, or accent.
>
> (Induction 40, 46-48)

In other words, *Poetaster* is figured not merely as a text, but as a classical text suffering from a disfiguring commentary: the word "accent," although not impossible for a text printed in English, most naturally is taken to mean the accentual marks used in the printing of Greek and Latin. Figured as a classical text, *Poetaster* is of the variety of comedy of which Sidney would have no difficulty approving. Even the audience are described as a "calme troupe" (57)—not the disorderly mob, but organised, ordered, and presumably proof against laughter. Jonson is simultaneously, indeed within the same sentence, creating two distinct sets of imagery to describe comedy: a literary set of imagery for his own work, and a second for his rivals which demonises them according to the terms of reference of Elizabethan dramatic criticism. This device has already been seen in *Cynthia's Revels*.

This imagery of text extends beyond the mere Induction. In its printed incarnations, both Quarto and Folio, but especially Folio, the play comes equipped with marginal glosses of its classical sources. And imagery specifically of classical textual exegesis turns up in the main body of the text too. At one point Lupus enters brandishing a paper of Horace's which he claims is seditious. In trying to put a bad gloss upon a good text, he is described by Horace himself as a "ridiculuous commenter" upon it.[39]

A distinction between, on the one hand, theatre in the *Poetaster* mould—classical, moral, satirical, and disconnected from the players—and on the other, theatre demonised as a vulgar, dangerous institution, is maintained throughout the action of *Poetaster*. It breaks out for instance in Act III, where Tucca is talking to Histrio the player:

TUCCA: And what new matters haue you now afoot, sirrah? ha? I would faine come with my cockatrice one day, and see a play; if I knew when there were a good bawdie one: but they say, you ha' nothing but *humours, reuells,* and *satyres,* that girde, and fart at the time, you slaue.

HISTRIO: No, I assure you, Captaine, not wee. They are on the other side of *Tyber:* we haue as much ribaldrie in our plaies, as can bee, as you would wish, Captaine: All the sinners, i'the suburbs, come, and applaud our action, daily.

TUCCA: I heare, you'll bring me o'the stage there: you'll play me, they say: I shall be presented by a sort of copper-lac't scoundrels of you: life of PLUTO, and you stage me, stinkard; your mansions shall sweat for it, your tabernacles, varlets, your *Globes,* and your *Triumphs.*

HISTRIO: Not we, by PHOEBUS, Captaine: doe not doe vs imputation without desert. (III.iv.187-203)

The Tiber divides good theatre from bad as the Thames divides Jonson's location, the Blackfriars, from the South Bank theatres such as the Globe. The naming of the Globe in this passage, and the *ad hominem* satire of the personnel of the Globe that follows shows that Histrio's theatre is on the South Bank, the base of Dekker and Marston.[40] Tucca and Histrio's expectations of it are calculated to offend all the standards of Elizabethan literary critics. It offers bawdy on stage and immoral sexual liaisons among the audience, "a horse fair for hores" in Stephen Gosson's trenchant phrase. It is mercenary, in that the financial implications of the play that they are proposing to put on are explored at length. In entitling Demetrius "a dresser of plays" Jonson achieves at once a half pun on Dekker's name and a slur on his qualifications to be considered a poet. The Globe is portrayed as the territory of the player, and of the poet-ape.

As for the other, non-Globe sort of drama, the "*humours, reuells* and *satyres*" which Jonson describes in terms of the names of his own most recent plays, no reference is made its actors; in a similar way, and for a similar reason *Poetaster's* Induction glosses over the question of how it is to be acted when the only actors it mentions are in the audience. In neither case is Jonson eager to associate such drama with mere players. Rather, North bank drama is here given a moral function, in particular as it reprehends the vice of Tucca and his ilk. Earlier on in the play, Tucca, together with Lupus, has made a complaint about just this sort of drama, a complaint rendered self-referentially parodic by the fact that it is delivered by a character in a stage comedy:

> Your courtier cannot kisse his mistris slippers, in quiet, for 'hem: nor your white innocent gallant pawne his reuelling sute, to make his punke a supper. An honest decayed commander, cannot skelder, cheat, nor be seene in a bawdie house, but he shall be straight in one of their wormewood *comoedies*. They are growne licentious, the rogues.   (I.ii.45-52)

Tucca's fear of the corrective power of satirical drama strangely recalls Lodge's description of the power of Old Comedy, a description itself translated from the *Satires* of Horace: "ther was no abuse but these men reprehended it; a thefe was loth to be seene [at] one [of] there spectacle[s], a coward was neuer present at theyr assemblies, a backbiter abhord that company."[41] This is an indirect link between Horace and North Bank drama, but the phrase "*humours, reuells* and *satyres*" establishes a stronger pattern of imagery. Within the play, Horace is accused of writing "*satyricall* humours."[42] As a description of the satirical output of the historical Quintus Horatius Flaccus, it's inaccurate: the theory of humours does not enter into his satires. Instead, it describes far better the recent output of Jonson. The verbal echoes blur together Horace, the elusive North Bank drama, and Jonson himself. Although North Bank drama is never displayed, it is linked to Horace; it's not linked to performance, but to the classical author and the classical text.

But Horace's status as classical author within *Poetaster* pales into insignificance next to the stature given to Virgil. In *Poetaster*, Virgil's work is presented as the acme of textuality. His "sacred lines" on their own command utter respect, are sufficient in themselves for any eventuality a man might face, and will last forever. Caesar himself falls silent when Virgil recites, and guarantees Virgil's work "hallow'd circumstance" for its reception (V.iii.166, 168).

Virgil reads a passage chosen at random by opening his book. The thematic relevance of the chosen passage on Rumour has rather overshadowed critical appreciation of the fact that this is a wry anticipation of the post-classical custom of Virgil's Lots, prepared for by the allusion noted above to the inclusiveness of Virgil's work. And this almost scriptural reverence given to the works of Virgil perhaps explains why the Apologetical Dialogue gives him—and not Horace—most prominent place in its description of the purpose of the play:

> To shew that VIRGIL, HORACE, and the rest
> Of those great master-spirits did not want
> Detractors, then, or practisers against them.
> (Apologetical Dialogue 105-107)

But Jonson does not situate even Virgil in an idealised vacuum: he presses him into service, and has him lecturing the poetasters on the importance of classical decorum. If Marston ever attended a performance of *Poetaster*, he would have seen a thinly disguised version of himself, being told off by a version of one of the most revered poets in the classical canon. *Poetaster* is not just an abstract statement on dramatic or poetic theory, but one constructed oppositionally and in a way that is deliberately provocative, with specific and derogatory reference to other living writers competing with Jonson.

In *Every Man Out*, *Cynthia's Revels*, and *Poetaster*, a coherent campaign is under way to present comic drama as worthy of serious literary attention. More surprisingly, an integral part of this campaign is the representation of living people on stage in the manner of Greek Old Comedy. More surprisingly still, as will be seen in the next chapter, Jonson's rivals disagree with him about the literary status of drama, and argue against him cogently and intelligently.

CHAPTER TWO

The Other Side of the War: Marston and Dekker

Jonson's comical satires can be seen as polemical plays about literature in general and comic drama in particular. The representation of real people in them is a central, thematic part of their campaign that comic drama should be treated seriously. In this chapter, I look at the responses to Jonson, Marston's *What You Will* and Dekker's *Satiromastix*, and argue that each of these plays may be read in the same way. Each uses representation of real people as one of its means of conducting an argument about the status of professional drama, and to argue *against* Jonson's insistence that comedy is fundamentally a matter of text.

It was Jonson's attitude that produced his 1616 Folio, which—as the truism goes—set the precedent and laid the foundations for the academic study of English Literature; but it's an attitude that may appear a little simplistic next to *What You Will*'s celebration of the ludic and irrational, or the stance taken in *Satiromastix*, which sees performance as a continually negotiated compromise, and mocks the rootlessness of uncontextualised text. Perhaps unsurprisingly, neither of these plays has been especially well served by the academic disciplines whose origins they mock. Neither has attracted much secondary criticism, and uncertainties still surround the texts themselves. With *What You Will*, the uncertainties are the unavoidable starting-point.

What You Will and Fantasy

What You Will is clearly a play with things to say about satire and comedy: two of its characters in particular, Quadratus and Lampatho Doria, discuss the subject explicitly and at some length. Specfically, mention is made of a current fashion for "railing" comedy, of a fashion for writing satires against named individuals, and (twice) of representing living people in stage comedies, so it is also fair to say that personal satire casts a long shadow over the play.[1] But any attempt to read *What You Will*'s poetics of satire and comedy must begin with making the case that there is or is not personation in the play. Most modern critics, led by Philip

Finkelpearl, have developed readings of the play that reject the idea that personation is present or that Lampatho Doria has any particular reference to Ben Jonson. Instead, they read the play as a phase in Marston's artistic development, a work to be read only with reference to Marston's other plays and not for contemporary allusions. This is a shame, because *What You Will* champions inconsistency and playfulness, and is ill served by readings that seek to impose consistency on it. In particular Finkelpearl, in his efforts to accommodate a play starring an "Epicurean critic" within the oeuvre of a writer with a known partiality to Stoicism, is forced consistently to misjudge the tone, and to see the whole play as an aimless and depressing satire upon the Epicureanism it appears to celebrate: a manoeuvre of the sort that dogs Marston criticism, an invocation of what R. A. Levin has called "The philosopher's stone of parody."[2]

Although Finkelpearl's reading is almost thirty years old, it has underpinned all subsequent accounts of the play. In challenging it, and trying to reinstate the idea that this is a play built around satire of Jonson, I'm also challenging the basis of these later accounts. There are two main arguments for identifying Lampatho Doria as a specific caricature of Jonson: the portrayal of Lampatho as a character, and the links with *Cynthia's Revels.*

Jonson himself certainly represented Marston on the stage in *Poetaster* and, it is generally agreed, in *Cynthia's Revels* before that. In the Apologetical Dialogue to *Poetaster* the Author complains that his enemies' plays (that is, the plays of Marston and Dekker) have been attacking him personally—hence his response in this play. Years later, in conversation with William Drummond, Jonson explicitly stated that Marston had represented him on the stage.[3] In seeking whether there are any surviving plays in which to locate Marston's satire of Jonson, one must consider *What You Will* a leading contender. In particular, Lampatho Doria, one of the two feuding playwrights in *What You Will,* seems to have many points of contact with Jonson.

Arguing about topics like this was the favourite method of discussion in the nineteenth century, when it was all too easy to draw false parallels between characters and personalities on the basis of trivial resemblances, so care is needed. Indeed, several Victorian critics sought to find Jonson in Quadratus and Marston in Lampatho Doria, although after the work of R. A. Small it has become accepted that if Jonson is to be sought anywhere it is in Lampatho Doria.[4] Lampatho is an enemy of Quadratus, and satirises him, and threatens to write plays against him.

Quadratus for his part criticises him for his railing, and insults him too. Furthermore, Lampatho's plays (as seen in Act V) are in rivalry with those of Quadratus. So Lampatho is to Quadratus as Jonson is to Marston, a rival satirical playwright.

Against this broad similarity, Finkelpearl puts a catalogue of biographical reasons why Lampatho Doria is not a caricature of Jonson. "Probably the most effective way to portray a public figure on the stage is to stress his best-known characteristics," but this is not done.[5] There are no references, argues Finkelpearl, to Jonson's bricklaying, or his background as an itinerant player, both of which would surely be gifts for any satirist, and which are used in Dekker's *Satiromastix*. This is true enough in itself, but his own examples show up the problem with using this as proof that Lampatho is *not* Jonson. He quotes, for instance Lampatho Doria's renunciation, near the end of the play, of his former self: "Lamp-oil, watch-candles, rug gowns and small juice, / Thin commons, four o'clock rising, I renounce you all" (1562-63).

It is true that in passages like this Lampatho Doria is pictured as a former university student: which Jonson, biographically speaking, was not. But Jonson's own self-fashioning as a scholar was so successful that the false idea that he had attended Cambridge was believed by Jonson's contemporaries and by editors as late as William Gifford.[6] And if we look at the presentation of Jonson or the Jonson-character in the three plays which no-one doubts to be involved in the War—namely *Cynthia's Revels, Poetaster* and *Satiromastix*—we find him presented in scholarly terms: indeed, terms which use precisely the objects named here. In *Cynthia's Revels* Crites is a "candle-waster"; "he smells all lamp-oyle"; and although not actually wearing rug, he is a "grogran-rascall"—wearing a similarly uncourtly fabric. In *Poetaster*'s Apologetical Dialogue the Author talks about the "pinching throes" of his writing endeavours lit by a "dumbe candle"; and the Horace of *Satiromastix*, "that Iudas yonder that walkes in Rug," that "staru'd rascall," writes by the light of a candle thematic enough to be specified in the scene-direction.[7] *Satiromastix* calls Jonson "self-creating Horace," and in *What You Will* it's the self-fashioned Jonson being satirised, while *Satiromastix* makes capital of the difference between the self-fashioned self and the sordid reality. This is the reason why *Satiromastix* digs up the stories of bricklaying and imprisonment, to create two contrasting versions of Jonson, while *What You Will* contents itself with the simpler and less inflammatory task of reducing Jonson to a single, unitary humour: the out-of-step ex-scholar.

Finkelpearl points out correctly that Lampatho does not obviously resemble Jonson. On the other hand, Jonson's "little fat HORACE," described as "pigmey" in *Satiromastix*, is no portrait of the tall and (at this stage of his career) raw-boned Jonson whom, in *Satiromastix* at least, the character is intended to represent.[8] So, perhaps surprisingly, physically accurate personal representation of the victim of one's satire was not put at a high premium in these plays. Finkelpearl also expresses concern that Lampatho Doria is not portrayed as "a professional man of letters."[9] But *What You Will* is very vague about how any of its characters make a living. They are all gallants, all—as Finkelpearl complains—on perpetual holiday. Insofar as Lampatho is a producer of court entertainments, he is portrayed as a professional man of letters, just as Crites is.

So Finkelpearl's point about personal appearance is irrelevant. It is not surprising that no allusion is made to Jonson's disreputable past. And the argument about Lampatho's career as a scholar tends to prove rather than deny the point. It therefore seems perverse to maintain Finkelpearl's doubts on grounds of biographical similarity, and one may conclude that Lampatho Doria does sufficiently resemble Ben Jonson.[10]

Secondly, *What You Will* has a relationship with the text of *Cynthia's Revels*. Indeed its reworking of some Jonson passages provides some of the best evidence for the date of *What You Will*. For instance, Jonson's Crites says:

> If good CHRESTUS,
> EUTHUS, or PHRONIMUS, had spoke the words,
> They would have moou'd me, and I should haue call'd
> My thoughts, and actions, to a strict accompt
> Upon the hearing: But when I remember,
> Tis HEDON, and ANAIDES . . .

The trope reappears reversed in the mouth of Marston's Quadratus, and is combined with a second *Cynthia's Revels* tag:

> Should discreet Mastigophoros
> Or the dear spirit, acute Canaidus . . .
> . . . .
> . . . once menace me,
> Or curb my humours with well-govern'd check,
> I should with most industrious regard
> Observe, abstain, and curb my skipping lightness;
> But when an arrogant odd impudent. . . .[11]

Another instance of the connection between the two plays can be found a little later in the same scene, and again in lines spoken by Quadratus. Among the things satirised in *Cynthia's Revels* as symbols of frivolity are anchovies, caviar, fantasticness personified as the character Phantaste, and extravagance in clothing and headgear. Thus, the following speech by Quadratus, whose praise of fantasy may be considered an epigraph to all of *What You Will*, takes its opening verbal cues directly from *Cynthia's Revels*:

> A man can scarce put on a tuck'd-up cap,
> A button'd frizado suit, scarce eat good meat,
> Anchovies, caviare, but he's satir'd
> And term'd fantastical by the muddy spawn
> Of slimy newts; when, troth, fantasticness,
> That which the natural sophisters term
> *Phantasia incomplexa*, is a function
> Even of the bright immortal part of man.
> It is the common pass, the sacred door
> Unto the privy chamber of the soul,
> That barr'd, naught passeth past the baser court
> Of outward sense; by it th'inamorate
> Most lively thinks he sees the absent beauties
> Of his lov'd mistress;
> By it we shape a new creation
> Of things as yet unborn, by it we feed
> Our ravenous memory, our [invention] feast:
> 'Slid, he that's not fantastical's a beast.
>
> (582-99)

Quadratus' praise of fantasy works by sliding together two different connotations of the word: "fantasticness," in the sense disliked by Jonson, and the fantasy as a faculty of the organic soul. In his general theory of the mind Quadratus is following Aristotle's *De anima*, elements of which were refracted through the three traditions of Arab scholarship, Neoplatonism, and Augustinian scholarship, and reassembled by Renaissance philosophers in a new form.[12] Although his argument is self-consciously fantastic itself, it is an accurate summary of the prevailing philosophical view, in which fantasy was an organ located in the anterior cerebral ventricle. It acted upon the data of the five external senses that common sense had processed, and converted them into "phantasmata" —images that were not mere copies of the outside world—which other organs of the brain, such as memory, could process. "Fantasticness," in that it is here given credit as the agency responsible for "a new creation," is made responsible for art: including the highly wrought and self-consciously showy piece in which this idea is contained, and including —as will be seen—even *What You Will* itself.

Theories of the organic soul provide something of a thematic key to *What You Will*. Elsewhere in the play, Lampatho describes how all his learning was in vain, with particular reference to his vain grapplings with the theories of the soul peddled by "Zabarell, / Aquinas, Scotus, and the musty saw / Of antick Donate."[13] In the main plot of the play, to which it must not be forgotten that Quadratus and Lampatho are merely accessories, the merchant Albano develops an uncertainty about his soul brought on by the fact that everyone thinks he is an impostor, merely an impersonation of Albano rather than the real thing:

> The Samian faith is true, true, I was drown'd,
> And now my soul is skipp'd into a perfumer, a gutter-master.
> . . . .
>   If Albano's name
> Were liable to sense, that I could taste or touch
> Or see, or feel it, it might 'tice belief;
> But since 'tis voice and air, come to the musk-cat, boy:
> Francisco, that's my name . . .
>   (1239-40, 1259-62)

The concept of the organic soul, and in particular of the interpretative power of the fantasy—which is lacking in both Lampatho and Albano, unable to cope with anything not directly discernible by mere "sense"—provides a unifying theme for *What You Will*. Furthermore, the same imagery of the fantasy occurs in the Induction, directly linked to statements about the nature of comic drama.

The Induction to *What You Will* sets up an opposition between two characters, Doricus and Philomuse. Doricus is a devotee of fantasy, something that becomes apparent quickly not merely through his direct mention of it but through his associative, imaginative manner of speaking:

> DORICUS: Marry sir, Signor Snuff, Monsieur Mew, and Cavaliero Blirt, are three of the most to be fear'd auditors that ever—
>
> PHILOMUSE: Pish for shame, stint thy idle chat.
>
> DORICUS: Nay, dream whatsoe'er your fantasy swims on, Philomuse . . .
>   (14-18)

Philomuse, on the other hand, is less tolerant of such unbuttoned frivolity. When he mentions fantasy, it is in a derogatory context, as an example of one of the things that an author should take no notice of in writing his work, along with things like the reaction of the audience:

Shall he be crest-fall'n, if some looser brain
In flux of wit uncivilly befilth
His slight composures?
. . . .
Why gentle spirits, what loose-waving [vane],
What anything would thus be screw'd about
With each slight touch of odd phantasmatas?
No, let the feeble palsied lamer joints
Lean on opinion's crutches . . .

(28-30, 43-47)

The important thing about Philomuse's speech, shot through as it is
with a vivid imagery of sickness that weakens one's confidence in the
speaker's self-proclaimed healthiness and calmness, is that it is a *reductio
ad absurdum* of an attitude of sturdy independence from the vagaries of
the audience expressed, most notably, by Ben Jonson in *Cynthia's Revels*:
"By—, 'tis good, and if you lik't, you may" (Epilogue 20). By contrast,
what Doricus has to offer instead is a view of art, not as part of an author,
but as a thing created by him:

Music and poetry were first approv'd
By common sense; and that which pleased most
Held most allowed pass; no, rules of art
Were shap'd to pleasure, not pleasure to your rules.
Think you that if his scenes took stamp in mint
Of three or four deem'd most judicious,
It must inforce the world to current them
That you must spit defiance on dislike?
Now as I love the light, were I to pass
Through public verdict, I should fear my form
Lest aught I offer'd were unsquar'd or warp'd.

(59-69)

The imagery is taken not from the body but from workmanship. Music,
metal stamping and carpentry make their appearance in Doricus' alternative conception of art as an artefact: something external to the author.
The author is deposed from a position of almost vatic authority to that of
a mere artisan who must obey certain standards of workmanship. Where
one might expect a Horatian stress on balancing the "utile" and the
"dulce," Doricus concentrates instead purely upon the "dulce." In addition, he rejects literary precedent in favour of "common sense." Again,
the vocabulary of the organic soul surfaces: common sense is what
provides the raw material for the fantasy to work on.

Doricus' tirade has its effect. Chastened, Philomuse lapses into prose. Doricus asks him the genre of the play they are about to watch:

DORICUS: Is't comedy, tragedy, pastoral, moral, nocturnal or history?

PHILOMUSE: Faith perfectly neither, but even *what you will*, a slight toy, lightly composed, too swiftly finish'd, ill plotted, worse written, I fear me worst acted, and indeed *what you will.*

DORICUS: Why I like this vein well now. (87-91)

The spectators' active role in creating the play before them is stressed even in the title. Doricus throws onto the audience the responsibility of generically locating the play, if they think it worth their trouble. In its refusal to conform to any of the genres into which Elizabethan critics such as Sidney, Puttenham, Webbe and Meres had classified all drama, this piece refuses to play by the rules of these poetic systems. As can be seen in Envy's Induction in *Poetaster*, a large concern of Jonson is his fear of allowing the audience the sort of creatively interpretative role that they are allowed—indeed forced into—here, in making what they will of *What You Will*.

Likewise, one of the differences within the play between Quadratus (who is most definitely not "unsquared") and Lampatho relates to the works of art that they create. Lampatho is unable to judge the correct moment and the correct audience for his literary output. He tries to spring sonnets on the ladies at an inopportune moment, and offers a play for the Duke's entertainment which is so inappropriate in its moralising tone that it is never performed. Quadratus, on the other hand, fits his literary entertainments to the occasion, offering to "suit" the Duke's ears with "a subject worth thy soul: / The honour'd end of Cato Utican." The subject of this entertainment is souls, as it offers a discussion put into the mouth of Cato on "the soul's eternity." Not merely is it about souls, but it will affect the souls of its hearers: "O these are points would entice away one's soul / To break's indenture of base prentisage" (1962-63, 1971, 1982-83). This drama by Quadratus wears its learning lightly, as a functional aid to its ability to please its listeners. It earns its justification through the pleasure it gives, rather than depending on its moralising force (a force which is nevertheless clearly potential—after all, the subject, Cato, is famous for his virtue). The entertainment (which like Lampatho's is, through the exigencies of the plot, left forever undelivered) can be seen as a synecdoche for the rest of *What You Will*, and an example of the ideals of drama which it seeks to promote.

What You Will, in short, uses imagery of the organic soul to discriminate "good," fantastic drama such as that praised by Doricus and Quadratus, from the stiffer, stuffier model of composition favoured by Philomuse and Lampatho Doria. Furthermore, this latter model is to some extent parodic of the classics-based, text-privileging stance of Jonson's comical satires. It seems likely that personal satire of Jonson is an important part of Marston's technique here, although, admittedly, the ludic inconsistency of *What You Will* means that the attack on Jonson is not in the transparent mode adopted by *Satiromastix*. But then, *Satiromastix* does not just offer a different version of Ben Jonson: it also offers a third intellectual model of professional drama to set beside those of Jonson and Marston.

Satiromastix: the Baiting of Ben Jonson

As with *What You Will*, so with *Satiromastix*. It's been neglected and misunderstood because it has been interpreted from a critical position with which it is not in accord. An example of this in miniature is provided by the question of its running-title—"The Untrussing of the Humorous Poet."

According to received wisdom, Jonson's *Poetaster* represents a coup over Dekker: Jonson rushed his play out before *Satiromastix* was ready, anticipating its characters and drawing its sting. Among the other details which it is assumed Jonson has scooped is the running-title of Dekker's play, since this phrase is used by Jonson's poetasters of the play that they themselves are writing. But there are some self-evident problems with this scenario. Fifteen weeks, which is according to Envy, the amount of time taken to write *Poetaster*, is arguably a short time for the notoriously laborious Jonson, but it would imply that Dekker's play had lingered in composition for longer still: and Dekker was notoriously prolific.[14]

Furthermore, all the satire in *Satiromastix* as it stands is crucially dependent upon the characterisation of Jonson as Horace and on the role of Captain Tucca, both of which Dekker himself freely says (in the preface) are themselves dependent upon *Poetaster*. As for Rufus Laberius Crispinus and Demetrius Fannius, one cannot even argue that Jonson has pre-empted names envisaged by Dekker. These names are combinations of those of bad poets mentioned in the works of Horace, emphatically not the names of choice for sympathetic characters in any setting, let alone the early mediaeval.[15] It is a sign of what Julia Gasper calls the "condescending picture" painted of Dekker by critics that it has been assumed that Jonson outwitted him so completely by stealing his names and his subtitle, when clearly the reverse has happened.[16]

The reason, then, that Jonson in *Poetaster* appears so well able to predict what will appear in "The Untrussing" promised by Demetrius and Crispinus is not that he knows in advance what it will contain; on the contrary, it hasn't yet been written. Instead, it's because Dekker sets about writing a play that will fulfil all Jonson's predictions and take on Jonson on Jonson's own terms, complete with a version of the man himself.

Satiromastix, in its printed incarnation, opens with a dedicatory letter, and a flurry of Latin that is not at all characteristic of the play that is to follow. The preface explicitly distinguishes the classical "true *Venusian Horace*" from "Horace the second," author of "*Euery Man in's Hvmour*," "our new *Horace*."[17] Taking material that Jonson gives him, and altering the context to make the material ridiculous, Dekker does to Jonson's assumption of the character of Horace what he will go on to do to Jonson's own words. For instance, he describes the conflict in these terms:

> I care not much if I make description (before thy *Vniuersality*) of that terrible *Poetomachia*, lately commenc'd betweene *Horace the second*, and a band of leane-witted *Poetasters*. They haue bin at high wordes, and so high, that the ground could not serue them, but (for want of *Chopins*) haue stalk't vpon Stages.   (To the World 6-11)

The literal meaning is ostensibly favourable to Jonson, but it is undermined by irony. The grotesque classical coinage "Poetomachia," with its implication of deliberate pedantry, would not appeal to Jonson. Neither would Jonson be so immodest as to call himself "Horace the second," although Dekker is merely stating boldly the parallel *Poetaster* made implicitly between the two authors; Dekker's strategy here is merely to report Jonson's claim, but in a way that makes it appear self-evidently hubristic. By contrast, Dekker's tone is casual, self-mocking, and far removed from the "high words" of Jonson's side of the quarrel. The imagery of a physical struggle implicit in "Poetomachia" is carried on in the next paragraph: "All mount *Helicon* to *Bun-hill*, it would be found on the *Poetasters* side *Se defendendo*" (To the World 20-21).

Again, Jonson would resist not merely the verdict here but the whole imagery of a fight. In the Apologetical Dialogue he refuses to state that *Poetaster* is part of a campaign: it's a once-only response to sundry impotent libels, a play of quite a different order to the material his opponents have been producing. Thus bringing in Mount Helicon here is a reminder of *Cynthia's Revels* (in which Helicon was prominent), and hence the fact that *Poetaster* was not so much of a one-off as Jonson disingenuously claimed. Dekker goes on:

> I wonder what language *Tucca* would haue spoke, if honest Capten *Hannam* had bin borne without a tongue? Ist not as lawfull then for mee to imitate *Horace*, as *Horace Hannam*? . . . neyther was it much improper to set the same dog vpon *Horace*, whom *Horace* had set to worrie others.
>
> (To the World 32-35, 37-39)

Dekker's assertion has been most fully investigated by Tom Cain, who locates a "captayne Haname" on the fringes of theatrical life in the 1590s, pawning bed-linen to Henslowe. Cain further points out that there was a family named Hanham with strong links to the Middle Temple, which—if this Haname may be identified as one of them—would make him, like Charles Chester, or like Jonson himself, a figure on the margins of the Middle Temple society whose influence on comical satire appears to have been so important.[18] All this is even more involved, since a Tucca of very similar propensities to Jonson's had appeared in Guilpin's *Skialetheia* of 1598, as an auditor of some bawdy love poetry, leading to speculation that all three Tuccas, along with a handful of other characters in Marston's verse satires, are personations of the same person.[19] The problem with this is sheer lack of evidence: we have no biographical information on Hannam to prove or deny the resemblance, or to explain why he should be accorded any role (let alone a central role) in a conflict between playwrights. The Tucca of *Poetaster* is, as Herford and Simpson note, a *miles gloriosus* with strong affinities to Captain Shift and others of his genre: so Dekker's allegation must remain "not proven."

Again, the central importance of personal satire to these plays is highlighted, but of interest here is less the truth of this particular allegation, than the question of why Dekker makes it. It is phrased as an accusation of plagiarism against Jonson—that Jonson couldn't have made Tucca without taking Hannam's words. Dekker has taken over Jonson's material, but the Hannam allegation weakens Jonson's claims to have the authority to make accusations of plagiarism against Dekker.

Dekker does not differentiate between imitating a person's characteristic language, and taking words from a text that that person has written. In *Cynthia's Revels*, one finds the same lack of distinction between normal speech and authored text, notably in the gallants' discourse made up of jests stolen indiscriminately from dinner companions and from plays. To the twentieth-century mind, though, these are two quite different categories of theft. "Imitate" is a pun that not merely indicates that theft of Tucca's language and of Jonson's text is equally fair, but also links the theft in both cases with personation. Jonson "imitates" Hannam both in copying his "language" from him, and in making a forged representation of him. Likewise Dekker acknowledges his appropriation of characters from Jonson, and applies it to personation of him, as if appropriating material from him were a necessary part of personation.

And "honest Capten *Hannam*" is a figure outside the literary world in which the quarrel has functioned so far. This indeed is the way in which Dekker uses Tucca: whereas Demetrius and Crispinus (themselves professional writers) adopt reasonably conciliatory stances that acknowledge the literary importance of Horace's potential talent, Tucca still behaves with the uninhibited freedom of tongue and lack of literary scruple that Jonson gave him in *Poetaster*. Hence Tucca is described as "the same dog . . . whom *Horace* had set to worrie others." The question of whether Dekker's Tucca still constitutes a personation of Hannam is left conveniently unanswered. Dekker goes on to insist that he is not trying to escalate the quarrel any further:

> I protest (and sweare by the diuinest part of true Poesie) that (howsoeuer the limmes of my naked lines may bee and I know haue bin, tortur'd on the racke) they are free from conspiring the least disgrace to any man, but onely to our new *Horace*; neyther should this ghost of *Tucca*, haue walkt vp and downe Poules Church-yard, but that hee was raiz'd vp (in print) by newe *Exorcismes*. (To the World 42-47)

The phrase "The diuinest part of true Poesie" is just the kind of rhetoric over which Jonson was seeking to gain a monopoly by posing as the representative of true poetry: Dekker refuses to concede. Similarly, Dekker claims for the "naked lines" of his texts the same sort of victim-status as that Jonson likes to claim for his: Jonson's Envy had asked her minions to "Shew your rustie teeth / At euerie word, or accent" (Envy's Prologue 47-48). And even Envy herself resurfaces, complete with snakes, later in Dekker's preface: "*Enuy* feede thy Snakes so fat with poyson till they burst" (To the World 51-52).

Dekker says that his lines need not be tortured, as they have nothing to hide. But even here, as in the *Poetaster* Apologetical Dialogue, the limitation of personal application is a self-undermining statement. The work proclaims itself to contain no hidden satire, but then cannot name the person it admits to satirising openly. Likewise in *Poetaster* Jonson insisted "I vs'd no name" (Apologetical Dialogue 84). At no point during the entire War do the participants name their opponents by their real names: the strongest taboo of all on personal satire, the reluctance to name names as Aristophanes had done, remains strong. As will be seen, even this decorum was sometimes breached in later satirical drama.

Finally, Dekker's comment about "newe *Exorcismes*" should be noted. A striking fact about most of the plays in the War is the speed with which they went from performance to print. Presumably such topical plays dated badly, and would not be valuable in the repertoire very long. *Every Man Out* and *Jack Drum's Entertainment* were published in 1600; *Cynthia's Revels* in 1601. *Poetaster* appeared in print in 1602, as did *Satiromastix*.[20] Dekker's metaphor describes a second, ghostly War, as the series of plays came successively into print. But even the imagery of the "ghost" to describe this has a polemical intent. In describing the printings of these plays as "Exorcismes" of something that was only properly alive on the stage, Dekker differs from Jonson. From *Every Man Out* through to *The New Inn*, Jonson's quartos present themselves as a truer version of the play than that which had been acted, in terms of extra unacted material, and so on. Dekker does not subscribe to this model. In this effacement, the lines no longer even have limbs to torture: they have become incorporeal.

This second War in print overlapped with and influenced the War on stage; for it seems at least possible that the parts of Clove and Orange, the objects of offence in *Every Man Out*, were among the new and previously unperformed material which Jonson claimed to have added to the 1600 quarto.[21] Furthermore, it seems certain—from the accuracy of his quotations from it, discussed below—that Dekker had access to a printed version of *Cynthia's Revels* while composing *Satiromastix*. Another unique feature, then, about the War in the context of Renaissance English drama is not merely the interaction between rival plays, but the interaction between performance and print. In *Satiromastix*, this opposition manifests itself in an attack on textuality of all sorts.

Dekker's Horace is first encountered in his study, composing an ode, just as he was when introduced in *Poetaster*, although in that play composition was an apparently effortless process. It's an appropriate choice of opening, not just because odes were the forte of the historical Horace. After all, the ode, the "simple, and continued Song" mentioned in *Every Man Out* (Induction 250) etymologically speaking underlies comedy, tragedy—and parody. The ode in this scene of *Satiromastix* is in itself respectable enough, and a good pastiche of Jonson, but it dissolves into comedy when we see Horace in the process of composing it:

To thee whose fore-head swels with Roses,
Whose most haunted bower,
Gives life and sent to euery flower . . .
. . . .
For I to thee and thine immortall name —
In — sacred raptures flowing, flowing, swimming, swimming:
In sacred raptures swimming,
Immortall name, game, dame, tame, lame, lame, lame,
Pux ha't, shame, proclaime, oh —
. . . .
Good, good, in flowing numbers fild with spright and flame.[22]

This scene is in fact a textbook example of Derridean deconstruction in the strict sense of the word — depriving a text of its monolithic power and unity by exposing the structures that construct it, and the rhyme-words that it chooses to repress, forget and reject.

A Derridean "logocentrism" — attribution of an almost divine stability to the relationship between signifier and signified — is perceived throughout as one of Horace's flaws. The ode, which at later recitations seems so spontaneous, is in fact a self-conscious act of writing. And it is typical of Dekker's strategy throughout the satirical subplot of *Satiromastix*: pieces of Jonsonian text, not just from *Poetaster*'s Horace, but also from Crites/Criticus of *Cynthia's Revels* and Asper in *Every Man Out*, are discredited by being uttered in farcical situations.

Satisfied with the finished version, Horace then recites the ode to his foolish sidekick and only ally, Asinius Bubo (for this version of Horace is deprived of the Augustan context and the extended circle of Maecenas so important in *Poetaster*), and they gossip and discuss the possibilities of Horace's social preferment. Other detailed echoes of Jonson in this scene have been recorded by Hoy, but the most important is this one:

HORACE: Why should I care what euery Dor doth buz
    In credulous eares, it is a crowne to me,
    That the best iudgements can report me wrong'd.

ASINIUS: I am one of them that can report it.

HORACE: I thinke but what they are, and am not moou'd.
    The one a light voluptuous Reueler,
    The other, a strange arrogating puffe,
    Both impudent, and arrogant enough.

ASINIUS: S'lid do not *Criticus* Reuel in these lynes, ha Ningle ha?

HORACE: Yes, they're mine owne. (I.ii.149-158)

This exchange can be set beside the corresponding lines spoken by Criticus in the 1601 quarto form of *Cynthia's Revels*:

> Why should I care what euery *Dor* doth buzze
> In credulous eares? it is a Crowne to me,
> That the best iudgements can report me wrong'd . . .
> . . . .
> I thinke but what they are, and am not stir'd:
> The one, a light voluptuous *Reueller*,
> The other a strange arrogating *Puffe*,
> Both impudent, and ignorant enough.[23]

The exactness of the similarities—apart from the confusion of "ignorant" with "arrogant," probably due to the word "arrogating" in the line above, and "moou'd" for "stir'd," "moou'd" appearing elsewhere in the speech from which these lines are taken—strongly suggests that this quarto was available to Dekker when writing *Satiromastix*, creating a unique interrelation of texts and performances.[24]

The significance of all these direct verbal borrowings from Jonson is revealed when Crispinus and Demetrius enter, in Crispinus' first major speech:

> *Horrace, Horrace,*
> To stand within the shot of galling tongues,
> Proues not your gilt, for could we write on paper,
> Made of these turning leaues of heauen, the cloudes,
> Or speake with Angels tongues: yet wise men know,
> That some would shake the head, tho Saints should sing,
> Some snakes must hisse, because they're borne with stings.
> (I.ii.204-10)

In these lines Dekker is rehearsing a version of the doctrine of "things indifferent" whose most famous reappearance in English literature will be in Milton's *Paradise Regained*.[25]

This idea insists that no object, or text, is so purely good that it is incapable of perversion or misapplication, not even the Scriptures. In *Paradise Regained* the Devil's persuasions are no less evil for being couched in biblical quotations, as words themselves do not carry an absolute value or power. The particular application of this idea to Scripture, reflected in Crispinus' imagery of angels and saints, is especially appropriate in view of *Poetaster*'s elevation of Virgil's text to almost scriptural status, as discussed above. Dekker's recognition that there will be no unanswerable answers—that not even the angels' song will get an unproblematic hearing—rejects the idea of natural language, viewing language instead as something negotiated by the parties involved.

In this scene, then, Dekker is undermining language's claims to be absolute, and hence undermining the Jonsonian idea that his play is an unambiguously virtuous text which must be protected at all costs from misinterpretation. Jonson fears the idea that the spectator is an active constructor of the drama they are watching—since at least part of the audience have "basiliske's eyes," and will try to "Peruert, and poyson all they heare, or see" (*Poetaster*, Envy's Induction 36, 39). Jonson wants a banished Envy and an inviolable text that the audience should passively accept, but the Envy in Dekker's Epistle is to die not by force but by her own poisonousness (Epistle 51-52). Dekker claims not to fear debate and dissent, seeing it as a process of moving towards truth. In fact, what Dekker proposes is a dialectical model of moral advice in general and satire in particular, in which "friends" can administer each other gilded "pills" for correction and improvement. This emphasis on reciprocity can be seen especially clearly—again in connection with the point about oaths—in Crispinus' next speech:

> Say you sweare
> Your loue and your aleageance to bright vertue
> Makes you descend so low, as to put on
> The Office of an Executioner,
> Onely to strike off the swolne head of sinne,
> Where ere you finde it standing; Say you sweare,
> And make damnation parcell of your oath,
> That when your lashing iestes make all men bleed;
> Yet you whip none. Court, Citty, country, friends,
> Foes, all must smart alike; yet Court, nor Citty,
> Nor foe, nor friend, dare winch at you; great pitty.
>
> (I.ii.227-37)

It is not merely that Dekker is denying Jonson a quasi-hieratic position as arbiter of morals: he is denying anyone that position. Dekker further rejects the Jonsonian (and Horatian) view that attacks on vice in general will not make the virtuous man "smart." Instead, he is constructing an audience of imperfect people, who do and always will fail to live up completely to perfect ideals, and whose attempts to do so are not helped by Jonson's caustic exposure of their shortcomings.

Furthermore, there is a repeated insistence on Horace/Jonson's overuse of swearing, reflected here in Crispinus' opening reference, and repeated a few lines later: "Say you sweare / And make damnation parcell of your oath." In the case of the character Horace, Crispinus has a point: even in this one scene so far, Horace has already made such oaths twice, both times, interestingly, in connection with his literary output. "Dam me ift be not the best [poem] that ever came from me," he says of the ode; and then a little later, "Dam me if I bring not [Tucca's] humor a'th stage" (I.ii.36, 132). Horace's "dam me" is the most powerful form of speech available, and the most dreadful oath one can make: it's an appalling thing to wish upon oneself, and besides, one can only be damned once. But, says Dekker, Horace/Jonson is using it and overusing it and not convincing his enemies at all. It is a point which the play comes back to again and again; Horace's swearing is mocked by the other characters in almost every scene in which he appears. Vain swearing is another example of the uselessness and powerlessness of mere language.[26]

Tucca's prose insults overlap thematically with the charges established by Crispinus and Demetrius in their blank verse. For example, Tucca warns: "That Iudas yonder that walkes in Rug, will dub you Knights ath Poste, if you serue vnder his band of oaths, the copper-fact rascal wil for a good supper out sweare twelue dozen of graund Iuryes" (I.ii.283-87). Again, the profligacy of Horace's oaths is under attack, linked this time not to debates about the textual status of scripture, but to an allegation of perjury; and this is typical of the way in which Dekker uses Tucca to provide a scurrilous biographical complement to the more theoretical and moral objections against Horace made by Crispinus and Demetrius. The end of this scene is a compromise. Tucca offers to be Horace's "Mæcenas" and to get Crispinus and Demetrius to provide scenes for the next of his "strong garlicke comedies" (I.ii.374, 334-35), thus insouciantly trampling on two of *Poetaster*'s main ideals, the virtuous patron and the idea of art as the product of a single, literary author. Subsequent scenes with Horace merely repeat this theme with variations, like *What You Will*'s satirical sub-plot and unlike the more linear structure of *Poetaster*. The stage action and the form of the chastisement may be different—the whipping with nettles, the stripping of Horace of his satyr's disguise—but the structure is the same. Therefore, these later scenes do not need discussion at length.

However, one later insult by Tucca is worth quoting in full, because it makes explicit the connection in the War between personal reputation and poetics:

Thou call'st *Demetrius* Iorneyman Poet, but thou putst vp a Supplication to be a poore Iorneyman Player, and hadst beene still so, but that thou couldst not set a good face vpon't: thou hast forgot how thou amblest (in leather pilch)

56

by a play-wagon, in the high way, and took'st mad Ieronimoes part to get seruice among the Mimickes: and when the Stagerites banisht thee into the Ile of Dogs, thou turn'dst Ban-dog (villanous Guy) and euer since bitest, therefore I aske if th'ast been at Parris-garden, because thou hast such a good mouth, thou baitst well; read, *lege*, saue thy selfe and read. (IV.i.125-36)

To take the last insult first: Tucca refers to the benefit of clergy by which Jonson had saved himself from the gallows, a custom over which Jonson himself makes jokes, trying to privilege literacy as a tool for understanding drama (see *Cynthia's Revels* Induction 39-41). This is mainly gratuitous muck-raking, but the rest of the insult is more sophisticated.

On a straightforward level, there is clearly capital to be made out of the fact that Jonson, whose *Poetaster* includes so much satire against players as a class, should himself have been an actor. Furthermore, Dekker seeks to associate him not just with the permanent professional theatre in London, but with the even humbler world of the itinerant play-wagon: "the originall Dung-cart" of wit, as Jonson later called it. It was a world that was also mocked in *Histriomastix*, the play that seems to have ignited the War of the Theatres, and which *Satiromastix* seems to refer to in its title. *Histriomastix*, it is generally thought, portrayed Jonson as Chrisoganus, an impecunious writer who is at least a little above the mere travelling players for whom he is forced to write: but this passage collapses the distinction and pushes Horace/Jonson down to their level. Even the role allotted to Horace/Jonson, from Kyd's *Spanish Tragedy*, is a piquant one. "Mad Ieronimoes part" is the very role—irrational, threatening, out of control—that Jonson himself repudiates as undesirable in, for example, the *Bartholomew Fair* Induction. In fact, one effect of Tom Cain's proposed redating of *Poetaster* and consequentially of *Satiromastix* as well to the later autumn of 1601 would be to make the Ieronimo reference exquisitely apt and topical, for in September 1601, Jonson was being paid to write additions to *The Spanish Tragedy*—that is, he was actively involved in the very play which is here described as part of his old disreputable lifestyle.[27] What is more, "Mimicke," if we may judge from its appearances in Jonson's own language, is an especially pejorative word for an actor.[28]

Tucca's use of the word "Stagerite" is a startlingly erudite pun. It's a nonce-word, a *hapax legomenon* even in the *OED*. The pun is on "Stagirite," an inhabitant of Stagira, a title specifically of Aristotle, and even this word is so rare the *OED* does not record it until 1620.[29] The rest of the sentence describes of course the *Isle of Dogs* incident of 1597, so the pun in "Stagerites" insinuates that the *Isle of Dogs* was a gross violation of artistic standards as well as being imprudent: that Jonson has put himself outside the pale of the theories he espouses by his reckless satire, and is rejected both by the stage and by the theorists.

Finally, Jonson is said to have become a "Ban-dog." This insult contributes to a pattern of imagery of bears and dogs which has been present since the Epistle, where the talk was of setting dogs on Horace. Horace has since been described as "Hunkes," the nickname of the bear at Paris Garden, and Hoy suggests "Guy" and "Fulkes" in the extract above may well be the names of bears or dogs. The imagery of Horace as a "*Beare-whelp*" continues to the end of the play (I.ii.319: V.ii.185). The interesting thing about this is that bear-baiting was the main rival of the drama in the competition for a paying audience. Indeed, sometimes, as in the case of *Bartholomew Fair*, the bears and the actors boxed and coxed in the same theatre. Jonson's later plays are full of contemptuous references to "the bears within" (*Bartholomew Fair* Induction 52-53), who become emblematic of bad entertainment. But one does not need to look past 1601 to find examples of Jonson's dislike of the bear-pits. In *Poetaster* he likens the "multitude" who listen to his enemies to "the barking students of Beares-Colledge"—Paris Garden. He claims to be uninvolved, watching on "Pleas'd, and yet tortur'd, with their beastly feeding": and yet somehow the emotive verbs hint at a weakness in Jonson's armour on this point which Dekker, clearly, is seeking to exploit.[30]

Bear-baiting, then, becomes a metaphor for the War as Dekker and his side would like to see it. Casting Jonson as the bear is calculated to annoy Jonson immensely, and to discredit his pose of aloof supremacy from any sort of combat. So this paragraph of abuse by Tucca in fact represents a well-chosen and pregnant set of insults that attack his personal credentials, but in a way that is focussed on poetics. Tucca also speaks the Epilogue, which serves as an epitome of the difference between Dekker's approach and Jonson's, and might almost be said to be part of a manifesto for drama. Jonson's original Epilogue to *Poetaster* is lost, suppressed, he says in the quarto, by "authority"; but whatever it contained, on the basis of his other Epilogues it is unlikely to have been as colloquial as that delivered after *Satiromastix*. Captain Tucca speaks it in characteristic prose (as opposed to the verse more usual in Epilogues):

Let's part friends. I recant, beare witnes all you Gentle-folkes (that walke i'th Galleries) I recant the opinions which I helde of Courtiers, Ladies, and Citizens, when once (in an assembly of Friers) I railde vpon them: that Hereticall Libertine *Horace*, taught me so to mouth it. Besides, twas when stiffe *Tucca* was a boy: twas not *Tucca* that railde and roar'd then, but the Deuill and his Angels: But now, Kings-truce, the Capten summons a parlee, and deliuers himselfe and his prating companie into your hands, vpon what composition you wil.   (Epilogue 5-13)

The allusion to the "Friers" is of course to the theatre of the Blackfriars, where *Poetaster* was played. Tucca is concerned with the theatre as a physical structure, with galleries and "two penny Tenants," and with rival theatres around the city: he is more concerned with the theatre than with the play, again a position antagonistic to Jonson.

Tucca is claiming that it was not the real Tucca who spoke in *Poetaster*; in fact, Tucca is alleging that Jonson personated him. The temptation is to take this allegation as evidence in favour of the Tucca/Hannam identification discussed above, but this is deeply problematic in view of the fact that Dekker would be trying to remedy the situation with a second personation. Also, the statement that Tucca was formerly a "boy," and has now grown—ostensibly a punning reference to the fact that *Poetaster*, unlike *Satiromastix*, was played by a boys' company—suggests that Tucca has developed as a character too: which would sit uneasily with the idea that he was a personation designed to reflect some external referent such as Captain Hannam. More plausibly, the allegation is cheekily retrospective, a final witty exploitation of the paradoxes of personation and plagiarism raised by Dekker in his preface.

As in *What You Will*, the success of the piece lies in the audience's hands: Dekker even falls into the same phrase, offering them "what composition you wil." The contrast again is with Jonson's parting shot in *Cynthia's Revels*: "By—, 'tis good, and if you lik't, you may" (Epilogue 20). Jonson's idea of an inviolable text whose virtues may not be appreciated by an audience is countered by an insistence that a play stands or falls by its audience's reaction.

Finally, this analysis of *Satiromastix*, personation, and the poetics of drama allows one to go back and reinterpret the main plot of the play, in particular the resolution, which has generally—and, I think, unjustly—been seen as a weak and hurried conversion of a tragic ending into a happy one. One notices, for example, that the scenes in which this conversion is effected are suffused with imagery of theatre. In short, King William intends to claim *droit de seigneur* upon the beautiful Celestine, bride of Wat Terrill, until she prevents him by taking poison. The King is appalled and contrite, whereupon it is revealed that the poison was only a sleeping drug and all ends happily. Imagery of drama appears in large quantities throughout this last Act, starting in the scene where Celestine and Sir Quintilian try to formulate a plan for the fatal evening:

SIR QUINTILIAN: I, heer's a charme shall keep thee chaste, come, come,
Olde Time hath left vs but an houre to play
Our parts; begin the Sceane, who shall speake first?
Oh, I, I play the King, and Kings speake first . . .
. . . .
But to my part; suppose who enters now,
A King . . .
. . . .
                                    Then he speakes,
Thus—thus—I know not how.

CELESTINE: Nor I to answer him.

SIR QUINTILIAN: No girle? knowst thou not how to answer him?
Why then the field is lost, and he rides home,
Like a great conquerour; not answer him?
Out of thy part already? foylde the Sceane?
Disranckt the lynes? disarm'd the action?

                                    (V.i.55-58, 71-72, 76-82)

So the meeting with the King is being rehearsed as a dramatic event, but it is a dramatic event without a script. Sir Quintilian and Celestine are trying to work out a script—perhaps even predict a script—but it's not one that they already possess. (One could contrast, again, *Cynthia's Revels* where all the gallants already have scripts worked out.) It's precisely because the conclusion of their scene *isn't* a foregone conclusion that they need to rehearse it to work out how it will go.

When the event comes to be played out for real, it is set within the dramatic framework of a masque: Terrill's party are wearing masks, and enter "two and two with lights like maskers." The King, too, believes that his interview with Celestine will take a dramatic form, offering to help Celestine through "the Sceane of blushing," only to find that he is addressing her apparently dead corpse and "none plaies heere but death." Thereupon Terrill seizes the moment in a phrase that is almost Brechtian in its treatment of the dramatic illusion: "Now King I enter, now the Sceane is mine" (V.ii.36, 48, 52, 54, 61).

But Terrill, too, is deceived as to the sort of drama in which he is participating, mistaking it for a tragedy. The true nature of the drama in which they are participating is eventually revealed by Sir Quintilian, who declares: "I am an Actor in this misterie, / And beare the chiefest part," and reveals that the poison is not really fatal and that the generic resolution is really that of neither masque nor tragedy, but tragi-comedy. In terms of the imagery used to describe them, the death and resurrection of Celestine are dramatic events. Furthermore, it is important that the scene is a performance and not a script, since King William's self-recrimination and recognition of his guilt are only caused by his erroneous belief that Celestine is dead—by the fact that he has been deceived by the dramatic illusion. Thus a play which will "wed a Comicall euent, / To presupposed tragicke Argument" is privileging the forgiving unpredictability of performance at the expense of text (V.ii.96-97, 113-14).

The same is true of the most glaring incongruity in the play. Everyone knows that, in the historical texts on which *Satiromastix* is based, Wat Terrill ends up murdering King William II. In unexpectedly converting the tragedy into a comedy, *Satiromastix* is rewriting English regnal history with an alarming freedom. (An obvious contrast is Jonson's *Sejanus*, weighed down with marginalia supplying textual warrant for its fiction.) Just as Dekker's Horace/Jonson is shown to have put too much trust in the power of texts, so *Satiromastix* ends by cocking a snook at the whole idea of a performed play being constrained by the prescriptions of historical texts.

In conclusion, this analysis shows that *What You Will* and *Satiromastix* pursue very different sets of poetics in their different reactions to the challenge of Jonsonian satire. Both, in different ways, attack Jonsonian logocentrism. *What You Will* actively celebrates the ludic, while in *Satiromastix* the relativity and limitation of fixed pieces of speech or text are treated more soberly. Whereas *What You Will* invokes ideas of fantasy and phantasmata to undermine the Jonsonian stress on self-sufficient decorum, *Satiromastix* uses imagery of drama and introduces a metadramatic instability. *What You Will* bypasses conventional poetics as far as possible; *Satiromastix* is prepared to mock them insofar as they underpin Jonsonian discourse, and use them offensively when they can help discredit Jonson. To Marston, Jonson is Lampatho Doria, an inept, pedantic gallant deaf to fantasy; to Dekker, he is Horace, an arrogant would-be laureate with a sordid past and a hardly less sordid present.

The resulting plays expose ideological tensions that lie at the heart of a struggle over what professional drama might be and might become. As playwrights define themselves more and more in oppositional terms, the War becomes an active force that pushes Marston into writing an Epicurean comedy, Dekker into broadening the intellectual and satirical limits of tragicomedy, and Jonson into writing *Sejanus*, the learned tragedy which he promised at the end of *Poetaster*.

CHAPTER THREE

After the War: Personation 1603-24

In the years following the War of the Theatres, numerous allusions both in plays and in other texts indicate that personal satire remained a matter of concern. George Chapman, in the Prologue to *All Fools*, datable to the years before 1605, was among those worrying about it:

> Who can shew cause, why th'ancient Comick vaine
> Of *Eupolis* and *Cratinus* (now reuiu'd,
> Subiect to personall application)
> Should be exploded by some bitter splenes?
> Yet merely Comicall, and harmelesse iestes
> (Though nere so witty) be esteem'd but toyes,
> If voide of th'other satyrismes sauce?
> Who can shew cause why quick Venerian iestes,
> Should sometimes rauish? sometimes fall farre short,
> Of the iust length and pleasure of your eares?
> When our pure Dames, thinke them much less obscene,
> Then those that winne your Panegyricke splene? [1]

Chapman is here entering a plea for limited "satyrisme," and suggesting that as with "quick Venerian iestes" the object of the exercise is to hit a happy medium between priggishness and obscenity. In particular, the "satyrisme" he has in mind is "subiect to personall application" in the manner of the Greek Old Comedians Eupolis and Cratinus: that is, satirical activity in the form of stage personation. The Prologue to *All Fools* alludes to a theatre where stage personation was a common occurrence, and where the "sauce" provided by such personation was a central factor in the appeal of such plays. Chapman himself is known to have written in this vein. His own credentials as a satirist include the lost *The Old Joiner of Aldgate*, a comedy based on the contemporary events surrounding the chicanery of a barber named John Howe in his attempts to marry off his daughter. So flagrant, detailed, and extensive in its personal reference was this play that it was the subject of legal action in 1603.[2]

Rivalry and personation continued to be important and linked forces in the theatre. The three *Ho* plays, for instance resemble the War of the Theatres in that each play is a riposte to the previous one, and in that personal satire starts to make an appearance in the latest play. Dekker and Webster's *Westward Ho* (produced late in 1604) was followed by Jonson, Marston, and Chapman's *Eastward Ho* (1605) which advertised itself as an emulation of that earlier play: Dekker and Webster responded with *Northward Ho* (1605) which features a character named Bellamont whose resemblance to George Chapman is far from coincidental. In particular, Bellamont's speech is studded with references to the titles of Chapman's works. Although the personation in *Northward Ho* is far more kindly than in the aggressive attacks of the War of the Theatres, nonetheless debates about different sorts of comedy are articulated within this personating frame, since one of the amusing things about Bellamont is his desire to turn life into literary drama. For instance, on his first appearance, he describes a walk through London: "It hath afforded me mirth beyond the length of fiue lattin Comedies . . . I would make an excellent discription of it in a comedy."[3] A running joke in *Northward Ho* is the collision between Bellamont's literary pretensions and the practicalities of everyday life, or at least everyday life as written by Dekker and Webster.

The Induction to John Day's *Isle of Gulls* (first performed in February 1606) alludes to these *Ho* plays and identifies personal satire and bawdy as two subjects that Day will be careful to exclude from his own play. Perhaps unsurprisingly, the succeeding comedy is full of both.[4] Nor did dramatists abandon personation in the years afterwards, as numerous references in correspondence of that period show.[5] This chapter discusses four plays that contain acknowledged examples of such personation: Dekker's *The Whore of Babylon* (1607), *The Roaring Girl* (1611) written by Dekker and Thomas Middleton, the anonymous *Swetnam the Woman-hater* (1617-19), and Middleton's *A Game at Chess* (1624). With these indisputable examples examined, only then will it be possible to gain sufficient perspective to consider the Jonson canon, about which allegations of "covert" personation are persistent.

Throughout the period covered by this chapter, satirical comedies such as these, and their habit of personating living contemporaries on the stage, were discussed with reference to Aristophanes. Chapman's comment on "th'ancient Comick vaine / Of *Eupolis* and *Cratinus*" has already been quoted. In a Cambridge University play datable to the first years of the seventeenth century, Thomas Tomkis' *Lingua*, an allegorical figure of Comedy is introduced who "is become now a daies some thing humerous, and too too, Satyricall, vp and downe, like his great grandfather *Aristophanes*."[6] A few years later, Thomas Heywood's *Apology for Actors* found it necessary to defend drama against charges of excessive satire by quoting Horace's praise of the salutary effects upon the audience of Eupolis, Cratinus, and Aristophanes, a passage one has already seen used by Lodge for this purpose. "I. G.," writing a refutation of Heywood's pamphlet, counters by alluding to the violent death of Eupolis as a proof that satirical drama is a bad thing. Finally, in 1633, William Prynne compares contemporary satirical plays to the practice of Aristophanes; but of him, more later.[7]

The Whore of Babylon and "Time's book"

At first sight, the first two of these four plays—*The Roaring Girl* and *The Whore of Babylon*—would seem to have little in common. One is a citizen comedy, the other an allegorical historical drama. But what unites these two plays, for my purposes, is their referentiality to events outside themselves. Both are faced with the problem of dealing with topical matters in a dramatic medium in which such topicality was discouraged both by civic authority and by the authority of most of the poetic theories of the day. Their two approaches to this problem are so radically different as to be polarised, and while they're not in direct competition with each other, the difference between them reflects and reconstitutes the battle-lines of the War of the Theatres.

But first of all, it is necessary to justify the assertion that *The Whore of Babylon* infringes upon the genre of satirical comedy at all. While it is true that this allegorical representation of events in Queen Elizabeth's reign, namely the conspiracies against her life and the Spanish Armada, draws its imaginative setting from the *Faerie Queene* rather than any dramatic or satirical source, it has so many points of contact with satirical drama that early commentators such as Winstanley classed it as a comedy without a second thought.[8] For instance, it represents upon the public stage real people still alive at the time of the play's performance in 1606. Among these, the "Albanoys" is a representation, with the details taken from a printed source (the confession of William Parry), of one William Creichton. This Scottish Jesuit had been imprisoned in the wake of the Parry affair, but was released and lived until 1615. Also living at the time of the play is Edmund Neville, the original of the "kinsman" and betrayer of Paridell. As for Ptolomée Gallio, Cardinal Como, represented in I.i, he died in 1607, the year after the play was staged.[9]

These three living people directly portrayed in *The Whore of Babylon* are relatively insignificant. But it also seems likely that Fideli, the leader of the Elfish fleet against the Whore's Armada, is in some respects a representation of Lord Charles Howard, leader of the British Fleet against the Spanish Armada, and former patron of the company who staged the play.[10] He was also a commissioner at the trials of both Mary and the Earl of Essex, which fits with Fideli's presence in the death-warrant scene (IV.ii), and he was still a power to be reckoned with in 1606, serving on the committee charged with trying the conspirators involved in the Gunpowder Plot. *The Whore of Babylon*, inescapably and perhaps opportunistically a reflection upon that plot, is representing on stage, albeit with affection, one of the most prominent figures involved in the consequent investigation. In short, like the other satirical comedies considered here, *The Whore of Babylon* personates living people.

As well as personation, the play contains avowed topical satire. Plain Dealing's attacks on corrupt lawyers, debtors' prisons, and other abuses are recognised even within the play as the work of a satirist, and similarities to Dekker's later writing (discussed below) show that there is nothing outdated or antique about the satirical material that Plain Dealing delivers.

The Whore of Babylon accommodates and justifies this topicality by returning to a division between text and performance. Unlike much of Dekker's other work—*Satiromastix* and *The Roaring Girl*, for example—*The Whore of Babylon* is very much concerned to present itself as a poem, a composed literary artefact after the fashion of a Jonson play. This process begins in the preface:

> The Generall scope of this Drammaticall Poem, is to set forth (in Tropicall and shadowed collours) the Greatnes, Magnanimity, Constancy, Clemency, and other the incomparable Heroical vertues of our late Queene.
>
> (Lectori 1-4)

This self-invention is a creative appropriation of Spenser's description of the *Faerie Queene* in his letter to Walter Raleigh, where Spenser gives an account of his poem's "dark Conceit" in terms of an allegorisation of "the most excellent and glorious person of our sovereign the Queen," and compares his work to the epics of Homer, Virgil, Ariosto and Tasso. Imitating this letter constitutes an assertion that *The Whore of Babylon* too belongs to a high order of literature.[11]

The same assertion underpins Dekker's defence of the liberties he has taken with the chronology of Elizabeth's reign. He argues that he writes

> As a Poet, not as an Historian, and that these two doe not liue vnder one law. How true Fortunes dyall hath gone whose Players (like so many clocks, haue

struck my lines, and told the world how I haue spent my houres) I am not certaine, because mine eare stood not within reach of their Larums.

(Lectori 24-27)

In using Spenser's distinction between poets and historians, Dekker is also echoing Sidney's *Defence*. At the same time he is problematising the relationship between himself and the players who perform his work. Other early Dekker prefaces, e.g. those to *The Shoemakers' Holiday*, *Satiromastix* or *If This be not a Good Play*, express no such concern about the relationship between the author and the player; indeed, no distinction is made between the author's intention and what is realized on stage, and as we have seen, the printed version of *Satiromastix* offers merely "the ghost of *Tucca*" (To the World 45). But here Dekker is distancing himself from the Fortune, by claiming not even to have seen his own play acted, and yet also by blaming the players for its failure.[12] The distance is both physical and moral. Dekker even finds himself subscribing to the idea of a pre-existing, independent text which is then mangled by bad performance: the text is his child, "being spoyled by ill nurses" in its incompetent production on stage. For once Dekker is arguing the supremacy of text in a way more usually associated with Jonson.

The Prologue continues this effort to redefine the play as something other than just another drama: it has "Matter aboue the vulgar Argument" and demands (very much unlike for example *The Roaring Girl*, as will be seen) to be received in silence by the audience. The audience are enjoined to use their "Iudgement, not [their] passions" (Prologue 4, 21)—they must treat the play as an intellectual experience, rather than be moved by it. Dekker's attitude of deference to the audience's expectations as expressed in, for example, Tucca's epilogue in *Satiromastix* has been replaced by a new and more aggressive lecturer's tone. This is a history lesson. The Prologue, like the preface before it, makes no attempt to deny that there is topical reference in the play, but emphasises the distance, not the closeness, of the events it is recalling. "So, winged *Time* that long agoe flew hence / You must fetch backe, with all those golden yeares / He stole . . ." (Prologue 12-14).

In summary, then, the prefatory matter asserts that this play is a heroic poem, recalling English history: it renders explicit the relationship of players to text, and lays down instructions for how the audience ought to experience the play. *The Whore of Babylon* privileges text over performance, and this is true not merely of the prefatory matter but also of the play itself.

Queen Titania's power, for example, is founded upon a book. At her very first entrance, in the play's opening dumb show,

> *Time* and *Truth* meete her, presenting a Booke to her, which (kissing it) shee receiues, and shewing it to those about her, they drawe out their swordes, (embracing *Truth*,) vowing to defend her and that booke.
>
> (Prologue 42-46)

Later in the dumb show Titania shows this book to "certaine graue learned men, that had beene banished" (Prologue 49-50) who rejoice greatly at the sight of it. The work is identified in the first scene, where the Empress complains that Truth has written "A booke, / Which shee calles holy Spels."[13] As an allegory of the Protestant innovations in vernacular Bibles, the prominence given to this book makes sense, but also it sets the tone for the play in a more general way. And at the end we find that "Time's book" is used as a general expression for "the course of history"; speaking of the shipwrecked Spaniards, Time himself comments: "Of them the world receaues / But what *Times* booke shewes turning back the leaues" (V.vi.77-78).

This metaphorical use of "*Times* booke" is conflated with the literal use at the beginning: Time's book, seen on stage at the start of the play, has prescribed and described all this from the start. And in other ways, texts in *The Whore of Babylon* reveal rather than conceal truth, while performance, from Dekker's own preface onwards, is regarded—on the contrary—with some suspicion.

The Albanoys, looking to see whether or not assassination of the Queen is justified, goes back to "my readings and beliefe setled by reading," quoting Latin to justify his point, and upholds this written instruction against the fallacious persuasions to murder offered by Paridell. The deceptive performance of Ropus is exposed by means of a letter that incriminates him and is brought on stage. Similarly Paridell's evil intent is proved by incriminating documents quoted in the play—as Dekker insists—exactly from their historical sources. In all three of these instances, immoral, Catholic, action is frustrated by truth contained in textual form. This opposition gives new piquancy to the Third King's celebration, in a trope not unusual among the Machiavellian villains of the Renaissance stage, of his skill at disguise and acting.[14] And this contrast, the identification of Protestantism with text and Catholicism with show, is linked to the fact that *The Whore of Babylon* tends to invent itself as text, not performance. That this identification is *not* an obvious or universal strategy can be seen by comparison with *A Game at Chess* (see below).

Another sign of the text/performance opposition is the lengths that the play goes to to distance itself from—in particular—"railing" satirical comedy of the sort popular on the contemporary stage. The most important character from this point of view is Plain Dealing. His name harks back to earlier traditions such as the morality play, identifying him as a plain-talking reporter of events. But in his subject-matter, and in his racy, punning register, he offers a version of contemporary railing satire.

> TITANIA: What are those Serieants?
>
> PLAIN DEALING: Doe not you know (mistresse) what Serieants are? a number of your courtiers are deare in their acquaintance: why they are certaine men-midwiues, that neuer bring people to bed, but when they are sore in labour. (II.i.60-64)

It is easy to show that this is not designed as "period" satire, the sort of quaint thing that an Elizabethan satirist might say. In *The Roaring Girl*, a few years later, the same phrases occur in the context of completely contemporary satire:

> Some poor wind-shaken gallant will anon fall into sore labour; and these men-midwives must bring him to bed i'the Counter: there all those that are great with child with debts lie in.[15]

The parallel was noted as far back as Dyce, but its particular value here is that it proves that Plain Dealing's satire is not "historical" but contemporary.

Plain Dealing is audacious in the way that he—a comic character talking about one of the staples of Elizabethan and Jacobean satire, namely what it's like to be in debt—is addressing a monarch whose near-divinity is insisted upon by the play. He is being fitted into the role of a licensed satirist; and he is able to tell the Queen the things that her "courtiers" have chosen not to inform her about. But a contrast is drawn between this acceptable satire and other forms that are not licensed in the same way: Plain Dealing condemns

> Other fellowes that take vpon them to be Surgeons, and by letting out the corruption of a State, and they let it out Ile be sworne; for some of them in places as big as this, and before a thousand people, rip vp the bowels of vice in such a beastly manner, that (like women at an Execution, that can endure to see men quartred aliue) the beholders learne more villany then they knew before. (II.i.108-15)

The contrast here is between Plain Dealing, whose satirical discourse is permitted, even encouraged, by the Queen, and these other self-starting, unlicensed satirists seeking to involve themselves in the affairs of state. Satire is seen as a matter of state importance, as is clear from the way Plain Dealing can share a scene with Titania. Even more interesting here is that the satire Plain Dealing attacks is specifically dramatic satire, set in a theatre "as big as this." Dekker, in *The Whore of Babylon*, is going to some trouble to condemn contemporary satirical drama in the professional theatres, in order to distance *The Whore of Babylon* itself from such entertainment.

This anxiety has manifested itself in references to other satire earlier in the scene: Plain Dealing at one point describes the ordinary as "your Isle of Gulles, your ship of fooles, your hospitall of incurable madmen" (II.i.88-89). Although on one level these are just picturesque similes, Plain Dealing is in fact quoting the titles of one, possibly two, notorious prose satires, and one notorious play. Sebastian Brant's *Ship of Fools* had appeared first in English in 1509, and was often reprinted. The *Hospitall of Incurable Fooles* appeared in 1600, in a translation from the Italian of Garzoni in which Thomas Nashe has been alleged to have taken a hand.[16] Day's *Isle of Gulls*, discussed above, appeared in 1606; another Jacobean reinterpretation on stage of one of the landmarks of Elizabethan literature (in this case a burlesque of Sidney's *Arcadia*), it is therefore a sort of sister to this play. And Plain Dealing's satire that alludes to the titles of other satires links to the paradoxical railing against railing, and the metatheatrical joke of a talking about a hypothetical theatre "as big as this" while gesturing round the Fortune. Anxiety about how close *The Whore of Babylon* is to satirical, personating comedy expresses itself in self-referential attack on such drama.

In contrast to such satire, Plain Dealing's satirical activities are licensed and legitimised. Indeed, the Queen is impressed by his work, and gives him an office to "looke through and through that our great Citie, and like death, to spare the liues of none, whose conscience you find sickly and going" (II.i.121-23). Satirists of the period—for instance, Jacques in *As You Like It*—often ask for such a commission.[17] Plain Dealing continues to be important throughout the rest of the play, exposing vices and providing witty commentary, but the legitimacy of his satire in fact depends on the fact that he repeatedly attacks satirists as a whole. Through him, *The Whore of Babylon* is denigrating performed comical satire even while engaging in the racy topical reference (and, in a wider sense, the personation) associated with it.

On the contrary, *The Whore of Babylon* is presented as a poem, a text. Texts, most of all "Time's book," are privileged all the way through the play. This programme shows up in one other unexpected place: the printing conventions of the first edition, where *The Whore of Babylon* has marginal annotations. Of itself there is nothing special about that— examples occur earlier in Dekker plays, for instance, *The Magnificent Entertainment* of 1604. But what is unusual is the style of the noting, which is unique in Dekker's dramatic work up to this date. Instead of simply a plain comment in the margin, the annotation, especially early on in the play, is keyed into its reference point in the text by means of a letter.[18] Significantly, this letter-based style of annotation is common in classical editions of the time, and in Bibles, where it is favoured because the annotation is so heavy that one frequently goes round to "z" and starts again. In the case of this play, this utilitarian consideration cannot be a factor. There are simply not enough notes, and the notes are not long enough, to make this practice necessary of itself. Instead, I suggest, it has been deliberately introduced in order to assert the literary credentials of the work, a technique which it shares with the quarto of Jonson's *Sejanus* (published in 1605). So the thematic imagery of the play, insisting that it is a "Drammaticall Poem" worthy of scholarly study, is reinforced by the quarto text's typography, even while the notes themselves decipher the oblique contemporary references and satirical personations. *The Whore of Babylon* is presented as something quite different from Dekker's other plays, not merely in terms of genre, but in terms of something rather wider than genre—its status as literature.

The Roaring Girl: "Stories of Men and Women"

In almost every respect, apart from a common use of personation, *The Roaring Girl*, co-written by Thomas Dekker and Thomas Middleton and printed in 1611, offers a complete contrast to *The Whore of Babylon*. The play shows disrespect for all the standards established by earlier critics for good drama. Again, one returns to that indefatigable straw man, Stephen Gosson, who identifies two evils about performed drama which are particularly relevant to *The Roaring Girl*. On the one hand, there is the question of sexual immorality. In Gosson's eyes, the theatre both presents bawdy on stage and offers a meeting-place that facilitates the venery and debauchery of the audience itself: it is "a horse fair for hores." Secondly, Gosson dislikes laughter, seeing it as an irrational force, a "blocke in the way of reason," one of the things which permits "outward spectacles" to "effeminate" men.[19] It makes them like women, without control over their own bodies. This in turn makes its way into Sidney's *Defence*, in the form of his distaste for the "scornful tickling" of laughter as a fairly low index of aesthetic worth and pleasure.

Laughter and venery are very much distrusted by the academic defenders, as well as the attackers, of professional drama, and are likewise condemned by Jonson. In *Poetaster* (III.iv.187-92) he identifies the stage of the poetasters on the South bank of the Tiber both with bawdy on stage and with the pursuit of illicit affairs among the audience. In *Cynthia's Revels*, he registers disapproval of laughter in the symbolic form of the foolish and allegedly sexually promiscuous character Gelaia. In short, one would expect dramatists adhering to the standards of Gosson, Sidney, Jonson and the like not to draw attention to those aspects of their own work that involved laughter or venery. But this is how Middleton's Epistle prefaced to *The Roaring Girl* begins:

> *To the Comic Play-readers: Venery and Laughter.*
> The fashion of play-making I can properly compare to nothing so naturally as the alteration in apparel: for in the time of the great-crop doublet, your huge bombasted plays, quilted with mighty words to lean purpose, was only then in fashion; and as the doublet fell, neater inventions began to set up.
>
> (Epistle 1-6)

The Whore of Babylon's Preface was directed "Lectori," to a reader, in splendid Latinate isolation; here the readers are figured as more numerous, more varied, and reading in the vernacular, and it is clear that they will have less trouble accepting the following play.

Apart from the praise of "Venery and Laughter," there is imagery of trade here. Middleton is reducing the status of a play-maker to that of a tailor. His stress on the impermanence of the work, its cultural relativity in the shifting world of fashion, runs right against Sidney's (and Jonson's) insistence on the permanence and imperishability of art. Not that Middleton thinks the published play is worthless, however. It is

> Good to keep you in an afternoon from dice, at home in your chambers; and for venery, you shall find enough for sixpence, but well couched an you mark it. For Venus, being a woman, passes through the play in doublet and breeches: a brave disguise and a safe one, if the statute untie not her codpiece point! (Epistle 11-16)

The play is a recreational read, not a morally improving one. It represents value for money, picking up on the mercantile imagery that permeates the Epistle.[20] Furthermore, it offers the titillating prospect of cross-dressing, or rather cross-undressing.

Recent years have seen a lot of work on Moll's sexually ambivalent status, and the way that her apparel transgresses both sumptuary legistlation, and Biblical warnings against transvestitism.[21] The allusion to "the statute" above has been seen as an allusion to Deuteronomy's prohibition of cross-dressing—a passage Gosson triumphantly quotes as part of his reasoning that stage-plays must be immoral: "Garments are set downe for signes distinctiue between sexe & sexe, to take vnto vs those garments that are manifest signes of another sexe, is to falsifie, forge, and adulterate," complains Gosson, apropos of the boy actors.[22] Moll threatens this same distinction in the reverse direction, and on this count too is an alarming figure. In these three ways then—laughter, venery, and cross-dressing—the Epistle is celebrating the play's transgression of the standards that are associated with "literary" drama. The Prologue follows up and reinforces much of this imagery:

> A play expected long makes the audience look
> For wonders—that each scene should be a book
> Composed to all perfection. Each one comes
> And brings a play in's head with him; up he sums
> What he would of a roaring girl have writ—
> If that he finds not here, he mews at it.
>
> (Prologue 1-6)

So *The Roaring Girl* mocks the idea that plays should be considered as "books": it appeals for the co-operation of the audience, deflating the idea that drama is necessarily a text "composed to all perfection." Instead, it stresses drama as performance. As for laughter, and for the ephemerality of dramatic appeal, Moll

> Shall fill with laughter our vast theatre:
> That's all which I dare promise; tragic passion,
> And such grave stuff, is this day out of fashion.
>
> (Prologue 11-13)

Sexuality, laughter, and ephemerality are the key themes of the Epistle and Prologue, and these are all qualities which distance the play from the approved models of drama. In the play itself, all the advertised qualities are present, and so is a tendency to threaten the distinction between stage and audience. As early as the second scene, Sir Alexander, who on a literal level is referring to the paintings in the "galleries" of his parlour (where the scene is set), also, it seems, gestures at the audience with a pun upon the "galleries" of the theatre:

> Within one square a thousand heads are laid
> So close that all of heads the room seems made;
> As many faces there, filled with blithe looks,
> Show like the promising titles of new books

> Writ merrily, the readers being their own eyes,
> Which seem to move and to give plaudities;
> And here and there, while with obsequious ears
> Thronged heaps do listen, a cutpurse thrusts and leers
> With hawk's eyes for his prey—I need not show him:
> By a hanging villainous look yourselves may know him.
>
> (I.ii.19-28)

"A thousand," it will be remembered, is the number of spectators said to occupy a theatre "as big as this" by Plain Dealing in *The Whore of Bablyon.* Since both plays were performed at the Fortune, Dekker's consistency is unsurprising. Any lingering doubt that this is more than a reference to the man's picture collection can be discouraged by reference to the imagery of "plaudities," and the detail of the cutpurse, and the theatrical pun with which the speech is introduced—Sir Alexander comments there is more space in his parlour than in the "inner room" out of which they have just come.[23]

Such a description of the Shakespearean theatre from the point of view of someone standing on the stage looking at the audience is striking and unusual in itself. But it should also be noted that the detail of the "cutpurse in the theatre," started here as a metatheatrical joke, is then taken up repeatedly in the fictional action of the play itself. Moll says of the cutpurses she meets in Act V, "One of them is a nip: I took him once i'the twopenny gallery at the Fortune." We learn that she is conducting an investigation into the theft of a purse from the Swan, and in a third reference to this specific combination of playhouses and pickpockets, she remembers how she often "in full playhouses / Watched their quick-diving hands" (V.i.283-84, 305, 319-20).

Other topical references to theatre in the play include a remark by Gull concerning having witnessed a fight between a "butcher" and a "great fellow" that seems likely to refer to a documented incident that took place at the Fortune not long before the staging of *The Roaring Girl.* And to further confound the boundaries between theatre and life, we are told that Gull's master, Jack Dapper, tries to imitate the manners of "the private stage's audience, the twelvepenny-stool gentlemen." In the social world of *The Roaring Girl,* theatre is an important and prominent institution.[24]

In addition, there is another type of theatrical allusion at work in which characters in this play imagine themselves in other plays. Master Openwork suspects his wife and Mistress Gallipot of intending to slip away to Brentford with their lovers:

OPENWORK: Pray tell me why
Your two flags were advanced: the comedy?
Come, what's the comedy?
MISTRESS GALLIPOT: *Westward Ho.*[25]   (IV.ii.135-38)

Openwork is comparing his wife, wearing a mask, to a playhouse flying a flag to show that it is open for business. Here, yet again, one finds theatre linked to sexual immorality. Mistress Gallipot's reply, punningly explaining their behaviour in terms of Dekker and Webster's citizen comedy of 1605, is not calculated to reassure him. A little later in the same scene, it is Master Gallipot's turn to describe the behaviour of characters in terms of a contemporary play—this time an anonymous comedy of 1594. Master Gallipot asks, apropos of the disguises being adopted all around him: "I pray, who plays / *A Knack to Know an Honest Man* in this company?" (IV.ii.283-84). Admittedly, it's not unusual to have a play full of references to dissembling and play-action—almost all Renaissance plays, from the intrigues of love-comedy to the Machiavellian villainies of tragedy, are founded on deceptive role-playing of some sort. But it is more unusual to find, as we do here, this imagery expressing itself in terms of reference to participating in other contemporary plays. For one thing, it damages the dramatic illusion very badly: they *are* in a comedy of precisely the sort to which they are alluding.

All this theatrical reference within the play serves, as the equivocal description of Sir Alexander's gallery did, to weaken the distinction between the stage characters, who have spent a lot of time sitting in playhouses watching contemporary plays and keeping an eye out for pickpockets, and the real audience in the same position. Very possibly, entrances from the yard further blur the distinction between the presence of the real Moll Frith in the audience (assumed, for instance, in the Epilogue, even if not always literally present), and her dramatic doppelganger, who enters through the audience: no proof of this can be put forward, but it is persuasively argued by Mulholland. For instance, at one point Moll and Trapdoor enter onto a stage already occupied by Curtalax and Hanger, complaining as they enter about the street down which they are walking:

MOLL: This Holborn is such a wrangling street.

TRAPDOOR: That's because lawyers walks to and fro in't!

MOLL: Here's such jostling as if everyone we met were drunk and reeled.[26]

Mulholland argues, on the basis of dramatic practicalities, and the way that the doors on stage have functioned in the scene up to this point, that this entry is in fact taking place as Moll and Trapdoor shoulder their way through the groundlings.[27] This attractive idea based on staging considerations is reinforced by the evidence collected here that the play already contains a good deal of allusion to the theatre as a physical and social circumstance of the play.

Personation and personal reference go together with this blurring of the line between theatre and reality, since Moll Cutpurse, the eponymous Roaring Girl, was herself a real person. This woman, more formally known as Mary Frith, is known from numerous other contemporary references. Reputed "whore, bawd, cutpurse, and receiver," habitual wearer of male attire, devotee of tobacco and bear-baiting, she lived into her seventies and had the dubious honour of a post-humous pamphlet biography.[28] Other references, including Nathan Field's *Amends for Ladies* (1609-11), in which she makes a brief appearance, although reduced to a vicious transvestite bawd, and a reference in Brome's *The Court Begger* (1640), confirm Moll's continuing celebrity. And in many ways the character of Moll is the one most associated with the important themes of this play—venery, laughter, and breakage of the dramatic illusion. She is "loose in nothing but mirth"—a pregnant phrase that associates laughter with sexual incontinence even while ostensibly denying the connection.[29] The precise implications of putting a real woman into a play so much concerned with female rights are discussed below in connection with *Swetnam*, a second play dominated by personation and feminism.

Finally, the Epilogue is concerned to defend Moll's reputation, comparing the play to a painting of her in terms of truth of representation. It makes a point of this portrait being free from "all those base tricks published in a book," an allusion to contemporary jest-books featuring Moll in more morally dubious adventures which also thematically links in to a metaphor used within the play of "slander's books" (V.i.345) and serves to differentiate the play once again from written text. The Epilogue offers the prospect of further confounding the stage and the audience, by the appearance on stage of the real Moll:

> The Roaring Girl herself, some few days hence,
> Shall on this stage give larger recompense;
> Which mirth that you may share in, herself does woo you,
> And craves this sign: your hands to beckon her to you.
> (Epilogue 35-38)

This idea of a theatre responsive to public reaction, designed to generate a shared, communal "mirth" which the audience can help to create, is much closer to *Satiromastix* than to *Poetaster*. The sense that the boundary between the stage and the audience is a permeable one, articulated at the end here, has been present ever since the second scene: Sir Alexander, in punningly describing the contents of his galleries as "stories of men and women," (I.ii.17) has raised the possibility—which the personation within this extraordinary play fulfils—that the audience may of themselves become the matter of the plot.

Bark and Bite in *Swetnam the Woman-hater*

The third comedy to be considered in this chapter, *Swetnam the Woman-hater, Arraigned by Women*, is unique among extant English drama of the period. Although other plays represent living people on the stage, with varying degrees of transparency, and *The Roaring Girl* goes further than most and identifies the subject in the title, only this one goes further still and gives the victim's name. How is it able to justify this most blatant of personations, and who was its eponymous victim?[30]

Biographically, little is known about Joseph Swetnam. He was born, according to back-calculation, at some date between 1565 and 1570, and his early life appears to have included time spent at Bristol. In 1615 he published a book entitled *The Araignment of Lewd, Idle, Froward and Unconstant Women*, and then in 1617 *The Schoole of the Noble and Worthy Science of Defence*, a fencing manual.[31] From this it appears he was working as a professional fencing-master, although he refers in passing to his experience in continental wars; and his death abroad, in 1621, may well have been a result of returning to them.

The Araignment of Lewd, Idle, Froward and Unconstant Women was the work that made Swetnam's name synonymous with misogyny. This book, deeply unattractive to modern readers, is an anthology of proverbs against and examples of female depravity, pursued with a remarkable single-mindedness and lack of discrimination. However, its popular success at the time was impressive. There are thirteen surviving seventeenth-century editions, and five from the eighteenth century, the last of them dated 1733, as well as Dutch translations. In England, it attracted three contemporary refutations, all of which appeared in print in 1617: Rachel Speght, *A Mouzell for Melastomus*; Ester Sowernam, *Ester hath hang'd Haman*; and Constantia Munda, *The Worming of a mad Dogge*.[32] Furthermore, it provoked an anonymous play, *Swetnam the Woman-hater*, acted at the Red Bull at some point between 1617 and 1619. This play itself saw print in 1620, and although it never ran to a second edition, later references attest to its continued currency even into the 1630s. Stimulating work has been done on the sexual politics of the controversy, and on the way that the replies to Swetnam permit or do not permit women to develop a voice in print and upon the stage.[33] I concentrate on a slightly different angle, namely how the play seeks to justify its personation, and how this leads it into many of the concerns shared by other plays in this study.

Swetnam is actually a play about a Sicilian kingdom ruled over by King Atticus. His daughter Leonida, on whom the line of succession rests, is in danger of falling into the wardship—and the matrimonial clutches—of the wicked Nicanor, chief adviser to the King. Into this kingdom arrives Joseph Swetnam, who announces that he has fled from England because of the hostility provoked by the appearance of his book, and that he has adopted the false name of Misogenos,[34] the better to repeat his success upon the Sicilians. His clown Swash, himself a closet womaniser, makes ironic commentary upon his progress.

Leonida is through Nicanor's agency betrayed in a sexually compromising situation with her lover Lysandro. Under Sicilian law, the offender in such cases must be put to death, but it is unclear which of them was the instigator. There follows a long forensic debate about the sexes between Misogenos, who attacks women in general, and the Amazon Atlanta (really Leonida's long-lost brother Lorenzo in disguise) who defends them. After the contest Misogenos is pronounced victorious by the (male) judges, Leonida is sentenced to death, and her lover Lysandro attempts suicide. Misogenos falls in love with the Amazon he has debated against, and is lured by him/her into a mock-trial by the women he has calumniated. His punishment includes being tied to a stake, pierced with pins, and muzzled. Meanwhile, in the main plot, all the apparently dead characters—Lorenzo, Lysandro and Leonida—return to life, to the considerable chagrin of Nicanor, who resolves to reform and is forgiven by the King.

Themes of misogyny and calumny in the main plot are well integrated with the Swetnam sub-plot which provides the play's title and distinctive flavour. In fact, it is the sub-plot rather than the main plot that is of most interest here, particularly the way it copes with the task of conducting invective against a person whose main crime is the production of invective. One complication in any analysis of the play is that the source of the story is a novelette, the *Histoire de Aurelio, y Isabelle*, published in a multilingual parallel text several times between 1556 and 1608.[35] In this, a similar sequence of events centering upon a couple caught in an illicit liaison leads to Aurelio and Isabel being burnt to death and eaten by lions respectively, and the misogynist being slowly tortured to death by a group of women. Crandall discusses the changes in his source made by the author of our play, of which the most notable is the creation of a happy ending, but the existence of this source makes one doubt how specifically Swetnam-like Swetnam/Misogenos is. The play includes a ready-made misogynist's part: perhaps it was just opportunism to bestow on this part, almost as an afterthought, the name of a prominent contemporary misogynist?[36] This may be partly true, but the analysis of the play in terms of personal satire still holds. Misogenos is not merely a generic misogynist, but is constructed around the personality of Joseph Swetnam, both from his own works and from other sources, and in particular, he is consistently and thematically figured as an author of texts against women.[37] The play's satire against Swetnam as a writer makes use of a differentiation, by now becoming familiar, between performed drama and literary text; and to investigate that topic it is necessary to start, once again, with the material that prefaces the play proper.

The title-page assures the reader that this text is the "new Comedie, Acted at the *Red Bull.*" But there is little contemporary evidence to shed light on the performance of the play, which leaves us with the perennial problem of to what extent this text really reflects the performance. A clear example of this occurs at the end of the Prologue, with two alternative versions of the closing couplet offering two alternative modes for the reception of the play. Loretta the maidservant is speaking:

> Be but you patient, I dare boldly say,
> (If euer women pleased) weele please to day.
> *Vouchsafe to reade, I dare presume to say,*
> *Yee shall be pleased; and thinke 'tis a good play.*
> (Prologue 14-17)

The second version of the closing couplet replaces a formulation that insists upon the audience's responsibilities for good behaviour *qua* audience, with one that stresses the literary nature of the printed artefact, and it is a reasonably safe deduction that this couplet is an addition in the printed version, and furthermore one intended to supplant the last couplet of the Prologue. This is a disturbing example of post-performance interpolation caught in the act that threatens our certainties about the status of Renaissance printed theatrical texts in general. For researchers, the two couplets present a horror story to put beside the insistent claim made by *Every Man Out*'s title-page that it does *not* represent the text as acted, and the bad quartos of Shakespeare that deliberately misdate themselves.[38]

The printed version differs not only in the means by which the play is to be perceived (read not watched), but in the way it is to please. The excitement of watching the efforts of the company, and even a slyly sexual come-on ("If euer women pleased") is to be replaced by a dispassionate pleasure and an enjoyment registered by the intellectual faculty: "Yee shall be pleased; and thinke 'tis a good play." But it is the first of these interpretations, an interpretation that says the play is basically a matter of performance, that has been in force throughout the preceding prologue, and will indeed rule the rest of the play:

> The men, I know, will laugh, when they shall heare
> Vs rayl'd at, and abused; and say, 'Tis well,
> We all deserue as much. Let um laugh on,
> Lend but your kind assistance; you shall see
> We will not be ore-come with Infamie . . .
> (Prologue 8-12)

This passage very much stresses the role of the audience as a participant in the drama, lending its "kind assistance" to ensure a correct result. The Prologue further portrays the play as a neutral space, a judicial hearing of the case where both sides can make their own decisions about where the justice lies. This portrayal also anticipates the play's courtroom scenes that give the play its legalistic title and the subject of its titlepage illustration. Such presentation is obviously a little disingenuous, given that *Swetnam* is as much an authored piece as the book it is attacking, but this potential irony is being ignored. Neither in the Prologue, nor anywhere else, is the author himself (or herself?) mentioned, and so impersonal in its authorial style is the play that no-one has yet managed to attribute it convincingly to any playwright. In a manoeuvre which is the opposite of the Jonsonian tactic of insisting the play is a text, not an event, *Swetnam, the Woman-hater* is going to some lengths to conceal the fact that it is a text.

This manoeuvre has a lot do with the the presentation of the eponymous villain Swetnam. A blundering intruder into the milieu of tragicomic Sicily, Swetnam changes his name on arrival to Misogenos, in order, theoretically, to conceal his identity. His servant, Swash, is unable to grasp Swetnam's new, classically significant name that indicates his misogyny, approximating it instead at first to "A sodden Nose."[39] The character of Swash will prove important in what follows: his stupidity is used as a foil to make Misogenos seem relatively learned.

Misogenos' learnedness and literacy are stressed throughout the play. He defeats a disguised prince in formal debate, and quotes Latin tags casually and appositely when he has done so. Swash's account of how he fell in with him criticises his honesty, but still shows him a learned man: Swetnam/Misogenos is "The best Clarke, / For cowardise that can be in the World . . . " And "He was in England, a poore Scholer first" who promised Swash's mother he would make her son "A Scholer of the Vniversitie."[40]

All of this contradicts the real Swetnam's own statement in the *School of Defence* (195) that he has never had more than six months' schooling in his life, a contention thoroughly borne out by reading Swetnam's work. What the play invokes against Swetnam—as becomes apparent from all the references to his publishing activities—is in fact an anti-intellectual prejudice, quite different from the strategies used in the pamphlets written against him. These attack the poor intellectual quality of the *Araignment*, writing it off as an "illiterate pamphlet," fit only for the "vulgar ignorant" or the "giddy-headed plebeians."[41] They criticise Swetnam's grammar, his factual errors, and his self-contradictions, as part of their assertion that Swetnam is educationally inferior to the gentlewomen whom he attacks. In short, they attack his ignorance and low social class. In the play, on the other hand, the character who is proud of his educational superiority and who despises "The credulous people" (I.ii.47) is none other than Swetnam/Misogenos. Part of the reason for this different attitude to Swetnam/Misogenos may be that this play is being staged at the Red Bull Theatre, consistently described in numerous contemporary references as the least literary, most populist of the London theatres. The Red Bull, like its neighbour the Curtain, attracted playgoers of quite a different sort from the self-consciously elite audience for which, for example, Jonson had preferred to write at the Blackfriars. These Northern theatres were the last outpost of the jig. It is for this audience that an attack against Joseph Swetnam the intellectual can be written.[42]

On his entrance it becomes apparent that Swetnam has already published his book in London—hence his exile—and is now setting about publication and distribution in Sicily as well:

> By this, my thundering Booke is prest abroad.
> I long to heare what a report it beares;
> I know 't will startle all our Citie Dames,
> Worse then the roring Lyons, or the sound
> Of a huge double Canon; *Swetnams* name,
> Will be more terrible in womens eares,
> Then euer yet *Misogenysts* hath beene.
>
> (I.ii.1-7)

80

He has already "writ and raild" in London: "How my Bookes took effect!" he recalls. "The little Infant that could hardly speake, / Would call his Mother Whore" (I.ii.44, 48-49). But now he intends to repeat his publishing success in his new home. The imagery of the "thundering Booke" is of a missile which one launches and which detonates a good distance away: Swetnam is divorced from, indeed ignorant of, the effect of the text he has written. Swash is not so lucky, having been beaten black and blue by women in the street for the sake, not just of his master's ideas, but in particular his master's book: "A Pox on your Booke: I haue beene paid ifaith," he complains. Swash, "horribly imbost" with scratches and bruises, is in fact himself figured as the victim of a printing, and offers to show Misogenos the "Characters" that the women have left on him (I.ii.19, 14, 30). Swetnam's printing is coming back to him in an unexpected form, the puns complementing the repeated insistence upon the written nature of Swetnam's misogyny.

His other project, from which much humorous capital is made, is the fencing school that he runs, a topic explored in the succeeding scene in which he entertains Scanfardo, his new pupil. Biographically, this has its origin in Swetnam's authorship of the *School of the Noble and Worthy Science of Defence*, a title echoed in Misogenos' celebration of the "noble science," and it is made an excuse for some fencing-related horseplay. There are other echoes, too. His frequent address of Scanfardo as "Scholler" repeats how the characteristic form of address in the dialogue sections of the *School of Defence* (see I.ii.108, 115, 128). But what will happen with the fencing is a miniature of the argument of the play as a whole: Misogenos is well able to discourse about fencing, but when challenged to a fight, he is unable to deliver. He is a master of text, but not of performance.

Further text imagery in this scene occurs when Scanfardo unwisely brings up the topic of women. Misogenos rails against them in a series of statements lifted more or less verbatim from the preface of the *Araignment*. Of these the most interesting are those using metaphors of writing to describe women's wickedness:

> If all the World were Paper; the Sea, Inke; Trees and Plants, Pens; and euery man Clarkes, Scribes and Notaries: yet would all that Paper be scribled ouer, the Inke wasted, Pens worne to the stumps, and all the Scriueners wearie, before they could describe the hundreth part of a womans wickednesse.

The passage appears in the *Araignment* as follows:

If all the world were paper, and all the sea inke, and all the trees and plants were pens, and every man in the world were a writer, yet were they not able with all their labour and cunning, to set downe all the crafty deceits of women.[43]

So Misogenos is repeating and exaggerating Joseph Swetnam's words, but not by too much. Misogenos' version is more stylish and more physically vivid ("scribbled," "worne to the stumps"), and he is more specific about the quantity of women's wickedness needing to be described, but the idea is the same. In short, so dire is Joseph Swetnam's own rhetoric, that the play is actually forced to improve it to make Swetnam/Misogenos more credible as an intellectual.

In fact, Misogenos' imagined literary project is a megalomaniac extension of what Swetnam has already started: both in that it is an inflation of Swetnam's trope, and in that Swetnam's *Araignment* is already an attempt to write the unwritable book of women's wickedness. The trope itself, as Grosart pointed out, is not a new one.[44] What is interesting is the way that this play, in constructing a thematic framework within which to mock Swetnam, is able simply to adopt his own words and insert them into a new context to make them ridiculous. Misogenos' final words to Scanfardo emphasise once again his role as a producer of text in general, and one book in particular: "reade but that, / I have arraign'd vm all," says he, handing his book to Scanfardo, "That all the World may know that doth it read, / I was a true Mysogenist indeed" (I.ii.177-78, 180-81).

Swetnam/Misogenos is next seen at the debate over who is to blame for the affair between the princess and her lover, where he appoints himself to champion misogyny. Although, before the debate starts, the noble characters criticise him for associating with only low women such as prostitutes, once it begins he is a skilful adversary, able to make the disguised prince against whom he is debating lose his temper. Amid more general anti-woman rhetoric, we are not allowed to forget the association between Misogenos and text, in particular printing. Atlanta (the Amazon) says Misogenos charges

> The supple wax, the courteous-natur'd woman,
> As blamefull for recieuing the impression
> Of Iron-hearted man, in whom is grauen,
> With curious and deceiuing Art, foule shapes
> And stamps of much abhord impietie.
>
> (III.iii.70-75)

Misogenos turns the argument round and argues that the fault lies in the "waxen-hearted woman" who is helpless to stop other men interfering with "The stampe imprinted on her" by her husband (III.iii.85, 87). Misogenos again is seen as a representative of textuality, making demands of immutability from an inherently mutable world.

Like everything else in the debate, the argument itself is nonsensical. Misogenos and Atlanta trade stale exempla of famously wicked women and men, and accuse women and men respectively of being cunning, lustful and manipulative. It is Atlanta who loses her temper, because the comic character Misogenos can maintain the illogic longer and more tranquilly. Only the peripheral comments are really of interest for the patterns of imagery they build up around Misogenos. He is a rhetorical fencer (a trope that is itself a rhetorical commonplace): "How can my Fencer ward it?" "The Fencer's Schoole-play beares it" (III.iii.81, 226). And repeatedly he is figured as a barking dog. The "Swetnam as dog" trope begun here occurs no fewer than seven times in the play: he is "a dogged Humorist," a "iangling Mastiffe," a "base snarling Dogge."[45]

To some extent this picks up the patterns of imagery in the anti-Swetnam pamphlets. For Sowernam (115), Swetnam "currishly bawleth," and the title of Munda's *The Worming of a Mad Dogge* encapsulates her attitude to the man. But even as a dog, Swetnam in this play is a figure of fun, reduced to a "humour," and as the choice of epithets shows, his bark is dwelt upon, to the exclusion of any reference to his bite. Even as a dog, Swetnam's ability to discourse outstrips his ability to perform.

The third and final phase of the career of Swetnam/Misogenos, after his victory in the debate, comprises his downfall and his revelation as a hypocrite, coward, and liar. The reason he is exposed is his lust for the "Amazon" Atlanta. But the woman he lusts after is really a man, a fact that adds comic value and more besides. A device far from unknown at the time—from Sidney's *Arcadia* through to more recent appearances in Jonson's *Epicoene* and *The Devil is an Ass*—it is epecially appropriate here because it offers a deconstruction of sexual difference. If the one sex can be mistaken for the other so easily, it threatens the power of Swetnam's clear-cut generalisations. Secondly, the Amazon, the "masculine feminine," offers a way of breaking the polarised sexual stalemate of the debate-scene. A punishment organised by women is at the same time made legitimate by the acquiescence of men—namely Swash and Lorenzo.[46]

Still flushed with his oratorical success, Swetnam/Misogenos is lured by the Amazon to a banquet, and here his arraignment begins. The judicial imagery of the Prologue surfaces in the *ad hoc* "Female court" where the women arraign him. As well as referring directly to a standard trial, "arraignment" also refers to the title of Swetnam's book: this is the arraignment of the arraigner. The reification that saw Swetnam's *School of Defence* become an actual school works here on the *Araignment* as well, as it will in the Epilogue when the muzzle from the *A Mousell for Melastomus* becomes an actual muzzle. At one point, too, the hanging of *Ester hath hang'd Haman* is also being seriously considered (V.ii.224-25).

The penalties and tortures to which the misogynist is subjected are, at first, mild. To keep him quiet he is gagged so that he can only groan inarticulately. Swash approves of this: "Let him be gag'd still: / Then you are sure what e'r you say to him, / He cannot contradict you" (V.ii.236-38). Swetnam's position now is the opposite of when he was first seen, having released his "thundering Booke," and unaware of the "report" it was attracting. Now, he is unable to enter into dialogue with his accusers, and indeed, when ungagged and offered the chance, he refuses, keeping silent when asked whether the books brought in are his. The univocal mode, of authoring a text and releasing it, is contrasted with the multiple voices, the dialectic process, of the women's court—a dialectic into which Swetnam refuses to enter. In this way too, *Swetnam* privileges performance over text.

The punishment handed down by the court is for him to be tied to a stake "And bayted by all the honest women in the Parish" through every street of the city (V.ii.332). Misogenos, whose punchlines even in defeat perhaps indicate a certain ambivalence towards him in the work as a whole, opines that this will not take long.

This bear-baiting of a man is an interesting idea. On the one hand, it's another role-reversal, like the arraignment of the arraigner. Part of the *Araignment* is subtitled the "bearbaiting of widows," and this was taken up by his pamphlet accusers. Speght calls Swetnam a woman-baiter, and Munda announces her intention to bait Swetnam in his turn. All of this gives context and point to the persistent figuring of Misogenos as a dog discussed above. But it is also strangely reminiscent of *Satiromastix*, in which the whole Jonson/Dekker/Marston quarrel is satirically reduced to a bear-baiting, with Jonson as the bear. The parallel is useful not as any direct indication of source, but because it gives a flavour of the associations of bear-baiting, as lower-class, and as a matter of pure performance rather than text. Bear-baiting is the most undignified, unliterary fate for an author that can be imagined, and *Swetnam*'s strange policy of overstating the intellectual power of the play's victim is leading up—in particular—to this deflation.

Misogenos is also to be punished with whipping and transportation. Finally his books are to be burnt:

> Call in his Bookes,
> And let vm all be burn'd and cast away,
> And his Arraignment now put i'the Presse,
> That he may liue a shame vnto his Sex.
>
> (V.ii.341-44)

This is a third role reversal: the arraigner arraigned, the baiter baited, and the printer of texts put in print. On the one hand, this order for publication could be seen as working in a trite, naturalistic way. A pamphlet account of his trial is to be written up, printed and circulated in Sicily (an equivalent of this happens in the source, as well). As such, it neatly parallels and controverts the decree of the first, male-judged court, which we are informed is originally in the form of a document (III.iii.252). On the other hand, the paradox here is that the effect of this order to write up the trial would be to make into text the scene the audience has just watched as performance. For a reader of the quarto, the situation is equally paradoxical, in that the text that he or she is reading is suddenly given a genesis within the fictional Sicily it describes. The Swetnam sub-plot concludes with this metatextual flourish.

The play's location now changes to the royal court to conclude the main plot, where King Atticus, himself "bayted" by complaints for the wrong he has done to women by sentencing his daughter to death, is rescued from his predicament by her safe return and the consequent happy ending.[47] Finally, Swetnam (and here "Swetnam" for the first time supplants "Misogenos" in the stage directions) appears as an Epilogue, muzzled. He apologises for his misconduct and pleads to the women in the audience for mercy. His final promise to them—which is also the final couplet of the play—reiterates both the fencing-motif and the stress on the written nature of his hatred against women: "And this my hand, which did my shame commence, / Shall with my Sword be vs'd in your defence" (Epilogue 20-21).

All this has shown that *Swetnam* is a play with a ready-made misogynist's part, but that this part has been tailored specifically to refer to Joseph Swetnam. Although he is primarily condemned for his misogyny, much of the imagery with which he is associated shows that he is also reviled as a writer of books and author of printed text in particular. In this respect the Prologue sets the play up as a performance, a neutral

85

space for action rather than an authored text. In short, the quarto printing by means of which *Swetnam* has survived as a play exists in a medium which, within that play, is presented very unfavourably.

But, in fact, the confusion created is even wider. One of the reasons that this text is so difficult to treat in a scholarly manner is the perpetual confusion between the historical Swetnam, his stage representation, and the play in which that representation occurs: between Swetnam, "Swetnam," and *Swetnam*. Here, Swetnam's *Araignment*, the starting point of the controversy, has already undergone a metamorphosis into *Swetnam*'s arraignment, while the pamphlet that the women wish to write about the trial would become an (imaginary) book entitled something like "Swetnam's Arraignment." By turning a possessive genitive into an objective genitive, the imaginary book mooted within the play offers, in effect, a punning gloss on the original title that reverses the sexual power relations implicit in it.

The "woman question" provides a common theme for both *Swetnam* and *The Roaring Girl*. They are in fact two of the most feminist comedies of the period—in both, women physically dominate men, expose their moral inadequacies, and end up on top. It is no coincidence that they are also among the most direct of the comedies of the period, in terms of their personations. Ann Rosalind Jones argues that women writers of the seventeenth century liked the dialogue-form because only in such a dramatised, particularised environment was it possible to undercut the categorical assumptions about the differences between men and women invoked in formal debate. I suggest that these plays, too, use dramatised form to destabilize such debate, while their personations of Mary Frith and Joseph Swetnam provide external, empirical referents which flatly contradict those assumptions (that all women are weak or all men are chivalrous). They short-circuit the relationship between the structures of rhetorical discourse and observed reality—in other words, they present on stage someone from the audience—and by doing so, are able to bypass conventional axioms. A consequence of this illusion of actuality is that the plays in question are presented not as authored texts conforming to conventional poetics, but as authorless events that ignore or even mock such poetics: one reason, perhaps, that until quite recently they have had very little critical attention. In short, the argument over the textual status of professional comic drama enacted in the War of the Theatres—a war whose effects are still being felt in academic discourse today—proves to have had a marginalising effect on the some of the texts now most favoured by feminist criticism.

S W E T N A M,

THE

VVoman-hater,

ARRAIGNED BY

W O M E N.

A new Comedie,

Acted at the Red Bull, by the late
Queenes Seruants.

LONDON,
Printed for *Richard Meighen*, and are to b. fold at his Shops
at Saint *Clements* Church, ouer-againſt .ffex Houſe, and
at *Weſtminſter* Hall. 1 6 2o.

Frontispiece of *Swetnam the Woman-hater* (1620)
Bodleian Mal. 197 (4). Reproduced by permission of the Bodleian
Library. The document being held by the woman to the right of the
throne may be identified as Swetnam's *Araignment,* brought on stage in
this scene of the play.

87

Frontispiece of Q3 of *A Game at Chess* (1625)
Bodleian Mal. 247 (1). Reproduced by permission of the Bodleian
Library. The strong association between textuality and the chief villains
of *A Game at Chess* is shown here: the Fat Bishop is pictured with a book,
the Black Knight with a letter.

A Game at Chess and "play"

[Middleton's A Game at Chess is] the only work of English poetry which may properly be called Aristophanic. It has the same depth of civic seriousness, the same earnest ardour and devotion to the old cause of the old country, the same solid fervour of enthusiasm and indignation, which animated the third great poet of Athens against the corruption of art by the sophistry of Euripides and the corruption of manhood by the sophistry of Socrates.[48]

Swinburne's description of A Game at Chess invokes another historical construction of Aristophanes to set beside the Renaissance scurrilous railer or the Fryean ritual-maker, but nonetheless picks up on the fact that yet again, personation is at the heart of wider political and poetic issues. More surprisingly, here too these issues remain linked with an argument over the status of professional drama.

The first, and perhaps easiest, objective in substantiating these claims is to establish the patterns of thinking about drama evident in the furore caused by A Game at Chess. Why was it thought that the play was unacceptable, and who was considered responsible for it? For these questions an invaluable source is T. H. Howard-Hill's Revels edition, which appends no fewer than thirty-two contemporary references to the reception of this highly controversial comedy.[49] The main cause of that controversy was, obviously, the directness of its satirical reference. "The whole Spanish busines is ripped vp to the quicke, and Gondomar brought on the Stage in his chayre," as Sir Francis Nethersole noted. Sir Edward Conway complained similarly:

They take the boldnes, and presumption in a rude, and dishonorable fashion to represent on the Stage the persons of his Maiestie, the Kinge of Spaine, the Conde de Gondomar, the Bishop of Spalato, &c. His Maiestie remembers well there was a commaundment and restraint giuen against the representinge of anie moderne Christian kings in those Stage-playes.[50]

So the first problem is the political one: it very much offends Spain, and incites anti-Spanish feeling among the English. One correspondent compares it to the notorious anti-Spanish pamphlet Vox Populi in this respect—so from this point of view its genre is merely incidental.

But the second problem is a matter specific to drama: the play represents several Spaniards, and worst of all the Spanish monarch, on stage and in doing so contravenes some "commaundment" specifically to do with the theatre. Frustratingly, the interdiction Conway mentions is not known otherwise. Rather like the Old Joiner affair, this passing reference poses provoking and perhaps unanswerable questions about the extent of personal satire that was permissible on the Jacobean stage, given the rarity of provable cases of it in surviving drama. Conway mentions four people being personated; but the play's allegory demands that Prince Charles and the Duke of Buckingham be added to this list, and possibly others too.[51] For this study, the precise details of the extent of the personation don't need to be argued over, nor do the mechanisms of censorship around it already ably examined by scholars such as Richard Dutton.[52] It is enough to know that personation is going on, and then to examine the ways in which it is accommodated. But the contemporary comments supply several other pieces of information that need to be considered first.

For example, the comments record a rumour that the players had somehow procured Gondomar's own clothes as costume for the actor who played him: "a cast sute of his apparell," according to John Chamberlain. The historical truth of this is unprovable. But it's a common theme in stories of this sort of personation; Nashe alleged that Harvey's gown had been stolen for this very purpose in a Cambridge University satirical comedy. The townsmen pilloried in another Cambridge comedy, *Club Law*, saw themselves represented "in their own best cloathes (which the Schollars had borrowed)."[53] Clothes, here, are credited with power over their owners in a way more usually encountered in the field of witchcraft. Of this more later.

Another recurrent theme amid the uproar is interest in the players as a financial corporation. Estimates of the amount of money being made vary wildly: a thousand pounds in the first few days, the equivalent of three hundred gold scudos a performance, one hundred pounds per performance, two hundred pounds per performance, fifteen hundred pounds in total.[54] Even where a figure is not named, reference is made to the players' aim being to make money. Players are assumed to be mercenary in their motives and collective in their responsibility—one correspondent raises the possibility of hanging the lot of them.[55]

For the Privy Council, however, the problem of responsibility for the play divides into two: the actors, whom they reprimand and ban from playing, and the script (the poet himself having wisely absconded). The players produce in their defence the text approved by the Master of the Revels. "They confidentlie protested, they added or varied from the same nothing at all."[56] The script-book is passed to Sir Edward Conway, complete with the signature of Sir Henry Herbert, for puzzled inspection. The Privy Council seek to limit the performance, but their concern —the part that they can control—is *A Game at Chess* as text. So much for the furore, but what about the play? In the various printed and manuscript versions in which it survives, is it presented as authored text, as the Privy Council saw it, or as if it were authorless performance, the view more favoured by other contemporary observers?[57]

In this connection it should be noted that "play" in various senses is given a thematic importance early in the play. Chess imagery, stressing the very stylised version of actuality that the play presents, and the orderliness of the play's conduct, makes its first appearance in the Prologue:

> What of the game called chess-play can be made
> To make a stage-play shall this day be played.
> First you shall see the men in order set,
> States and their pawns, when both the sides are met,
> The Houses well distinguished; in the game
> Some men entrapped and taken, to their shame,
> Rewarded by their play, and in the close
> You shall see checkmate given to virtue's foes.
> But the fairest jewel that our hopes can deck
> Is so to play our game to avoid your check.
>
> (Prologue 1-10)

What is stressed here is the orderliness of the play that will follow. The formations are pre-arranged: the two sides are "well distinguished." This is a performance, not a text. But it's a performance conducted in accord with a strict set of rules. The game is fair and the characters who fail are not victims of forces beyond their control, but "rewarded by their play." Work by Paul Yachnin has revealed the homiletic contexts of chess allegory: contexts which stress the impersonality and inevitability of chess-rules as in, for instance, the trope of life as a chess game played against death.[58]

On the other hand, as Jerzy Limon points out, these very rules are broken throughout the play itself. Indeed, the Black House never obeys rules of any sort, ethical, religious, or legal, let alone chess-rules. And it is the Black House, more than the White House, that uses the word "play" and its cognates to describe the activity of the game. So within *A Game at Chess* there is a tension between the orderly ideal of chess in the abstract, and the deceptive, rule-breaking activity of one of the sides. In this tension the ambiguous word "play" has a key role.[59]

But as well as "play," *A Game at Chess* is also obsessed with texts, books, letters, and printing. Documents appear physically on stage from the

91

first scene onwards, and letters appear in each of the first four scenes. In the first scene, having failed to corrupt the White Queen's Pawn by conversing with her, the Black Bishop's Pawn realises that something more is required:

> My old means I must fly to, yes, 'tis it.
> [*Gives a book*] Please you peruse this small tract of obedience,
> 'Twill help you forward well.
>
> (I.i.188-90)

The stage-direction is editorial, but self-supplying: the book will physically reappear on stage in II.i, where the White Queen's Pawn is reading from it and it is luring her further into trouble. Unlike Truth's book which appeared in the first scene of *The Whore of Babylon*, this Catholic book is a force for untruth. Later in the first scene, the Black Bishop's pawn hands the Black Knight five letters, one by one, from the Jesuit missions around Europe. Jokes are made about the physical properties of the letters as documents. The Italian despatch is written backwards, reflecting upon the Italian reputation for buggery. The German one is sealed with "butter"—a reference to Nathaniel Butter the newsmonger that looks forward to the flood of Butter references in Jonson's *The Staple of News* the following year.[60]

In the next scene, the Black Bishop's Pawn picks up a note addressed to him which instructs him to rape the White Queen's Pawn; in addition, his entire cabinet of intelligences and love-letters, in which sexual and religious corruption are again entwined with text, is brought on stage to be examined by the Black Bishop and the Black Knight. In the scene after that, the Black Knight's antedated letters that provide the Black Bishop's Pawn with a false alibi against the accusations of rape are brought onto the stage and delivered to the White King. In the fourth scene of the play, the Black Knight gives the Fat Bishop a letter purportedly from Cardinal Paulus.[61] The letters of the Black House cannot even be trusted as to their content. Two of the letters that shape the plotting of the opening scenes are, in themselves, deliberately mendacious. Both the falsely antedated letter that is concocted solely to deceive the court, and the forged letter handed to the Fat Bishop, are intended to convey false information to the unsuspecting reader.

This profusion of letters is written exclusively by the Black side, and especially by the Black Knight—one of the two characters in the play who is an elaborate and fully-developed personation of a living individual, in this case the Spanish diplomat Gondomar. In the Black House, letters are associated with lust; and this is not surprising, in the light of Howard-Hill's observation that lust is the driving force behind many of the Black side's actions.[62] In addition, many of the letters in this play are associated with intelligencing and treason. To the references above, we can add the Black Knight's practice of passing intelligence to and from England inside "Letters conveyed in rolls, tobacco-balls," his plan to leave the charred remains of letters behind him to delude investigators, and his collection of maps and catalogues.[63]

Having argued that textuality in the form of letters is associated most of all with the Black Knight (Gondomar), I'd now like to argue that the other character in the play who is an extensive and elaborate persona-tion, the Fat Bishop, is also associated with textuality, but in a different form: he is linked not so much with letters, as with books. The Fat Bishop is a caricature of Antonio de Dominis, Bishop of Spalato, and bears the same sort of resemblance to his original as Misogenos does to Joseph Swetnam.[64] Whereas Misogenos was reduced to three humours, mis-ogyny, fencing and producing books, the Fat Bishop is similarly con-ceived in terms of religious hypocrisy, gluttony and book production. This becomes evident at his first entry, where after ten lines of talk about his corpulency and unholiness, his attention switches to his books, currently in preparation at the printing house:

FAT BISHOP: Are my books printed, Pawn? My last invectives
Against the Black House?

FAT BISHOP'S PAWN: Ready for publication, sir,
For I saw perfect books this morning.

FAT BISHOP: Fetch me a few which I will instantly
Distribute 'mongst the White House.   (II.ii.13-18)

The parallel with Misogenos is quite striking. He too is presented as a producer of printed invective, strangely unaware of what is happening to the text he has authored. The "fat and fulsome" volumes duly appear on stage to be handed out, one of a number of references that associate his fatness and his books together directly: as he himself says, "I have writ this book out of the strength and marrow / Of six and thirty dishes at a meal" (II.ii.21-22). Middleton figures the Fat Bishop's literary produc-tion as some kind of bodily secretion.

The most frightening thing about the Fat Bishop is the ease with which he, his body, and his books, can change sides. As he muses, contemplating returning to the Black House,

It is but penning
Another recantation, and inventing
Two or three bitter books against the White House
And then I'm in a't'other side again
As firm as e'er I was, as fat and flourishing.

(III.i.50-54)

In the world of *A Game at Chess*, text is shifting, unreliable. As the White Queen's Pawn puts it, in a rare White House reference to the act of writing, "What certainty is in our blood or state? / What we still write is blotted out by fate" (III.iii.57-58). The Fat Bishop, producer of shifting texts, is himself undone by a deceptive text, in the form of the letter ostensibly from Cardinal Paulus. As for his own untrustworthy books, they look back to the book of devotion given by the Black Bishop's Pawn in I.i and forward to the third and final book featured in the play, which the Fat Bishop enters holding at IV.ii.80: *Taxa Poenitentiaria*.

Taxa Poenitentiaria, the book of general pardons, is the excuse for some rather weak jokes about various sins; two of which (like the jokes about the letters in I.i) dwell on the physical properties of *Taxa Poenitentiaria* as a document. Adultery is to be found by turning the sheet over, while the penalty for sodomy ought to be written on the back cover. The rules themselves, open to interpretation, are a "cabalistic bloody riddle" in the words of the Black Knight's Pawn (IV.ii.130). The book puns and references draw attention to the fact that these absurd, equivocating rules are in textual form. *Taxa Poenitentiaria* is also the most deceiving book of all, since in *A Game at Chess*, the "bag" permits no forgiveness for the sins busily committed by the Black House.

Are there then any favourable references to books or letters in the play? The White King, praising the noble actions of the White Knight, refers to a metaphorical "white book of the defence of virgins / Where the clear fame of all preserving knights / Are to eternal memory consecrated" (III.i.162-64). The Black Knight refers to the "pestilent pamphlets" produced against his house in terms vague enough to include Protestant writers in general rather than just specifically the Fat Bishop (II.ii.98). Otherwise, letters or books are mentioned in the context of the Black House or the Fat Bishop.

References to text, then, are overwhelmingly unfavourable and associated with villainy, even in the case of metaphorical uses. Against the one favourable vague reference to the "white book" cited above, one can put the White Queen's Pawn's comment upon the words being spoken by the Black Bishop's Pawn:

　　　　　　　　So hot-burning
　　The syllables of sin fly from his lips,
　　As if the letter came new cast from hell.
　　　　　　　　(V.ii.42-44)

Hell, in her imagination, is a sort of giant print foundry. But as her conflation of spoken word and printed letter suggests, the definition of untrustworthy text runs wider than merely print. All forms of textual over-production, any attempts to varnish language, are suspect. As Michael McCanles has pointed out, Renaissance theorists on rhetoric and poetics tended to assume that rhetoric was indeed an external accretion upon an underlying "plain" meaning,[65] and in this light even rhetorical speech is a form of textual embellishment. And while the White House generally speaks in what has been called Middleton's characteristic "spare and primarily denotative" language, the Black House is far more inventive.[66] All the poems, orations, and incantations in *A Game at Chess* are associated with the Black House, and they all contribute in some way or other to its deceptive machinations. The Black Queen's Pawn, for example, uses a mock incantation to deceive the White Queen's Pawn into thinking she is observing a magic ceremony. The Black House's attempts to win over the White Knight and the White Duke feature, in quick succession, a Latin oration, a song, and a display of dancing statues. All these share the ulterior motive of seeking to convince the White Knight and the White Duke of the superiority of the Black House, with the aim of making them change sides.[67]

Here the imagery denigrating text starts to link up with the imagery denigrating playing noticed above. In one important speech, the White Queen's Pawn complains that the Black Bishop's Pawn is a hypocrite, because there is a clear disjunction between what he says and how he says it:

> If I might counsel you, you never should speak
> The language of unchasteness in that habit;
> You would not think how ill it does with you.
> The world's a stage on which all parts are played:
> You'd count it strange to have a devil
> Presented there not in a devil's shape,
> Or, wanting one, to send him out in yours;
> You'd rail at that for an absurdity
> No college e'er committed. For decorum's sake then,
> For pity's cause, for sacred virtue's honour,
> If you'll persist still in your devil's part,
> Present him as you should do, and let one

That carries up the goodness of the play
Come in that habit, and I'll speak with him;
Then will the parts be fitted and the spectators
Know which is which. They must have cunning judgements
To find it else, for such a one as you
Is able to deceive a mighty auditory;
Nay, those you have seduced, if there be any
In the assembly, when they see what manner
You play your game with me, they cannot love you.

(V.ii.16-36)

The speech begins with the metaphor of the world as a stage, a trope often used homiletically, as appears to be the case here.[68] And there is an exquisite ironic effect in a character in *A Game at Chess* complaining about a hypothetical play for which people have obtained other people's clothes. Regardless of whether or not the players really had obtained a suit of Gondomar's apparel, as John Chamberlain suggested (see above), the rumour was widely believed that they had. This play is an act of disguising of just the sort which the White Queen's Pawn condemns here.

The irony is compounded by the phrase "no college e'er committed." Howard-Hill, for one, sees this as a reference to the plays put on by the Jesuit Colleges at places like St. Omer and Douay. If this is the case, then what associations does this reference call up? The plays in these colleges were thought to be devoted to scandalous representations of the political affairs of Britain. Most famous was the play put on at the Jesuit College of Lyons in 1607, a sort of opposite number to *The Whore of Babylon* that celebrated the plotters of the Gunpowder Plot, as well as putting on stage such villains as Calvin, Luther, Beza, and Queen Elizabeth, and dispatching them to Hell, while rewarding the Popes and Saints with the joys of Paradise. This play was interrupted by a storm, and Protestant controversialists alleged that the abbess playing the Virgin Mary and some of the other cast members disappeared in the storm and were never seen again: it provoked at least five pamphlets in England that year.[69] The similarities in content between such plays and *A Game at Chess* are obvious. Again, *A Game at Chess* is very close to the very thing condemned by the play's representative of virtue.

In her insistence on old-fashioned standards of representational sobriety, the White Queen's Pawn reminds one very much of Sidney's *Defence*: particularly in her idea that characters can be divided into fixed and established types, and that these types can be identified and "read" by means of certain marks. In Sidney's words,

We get as it were an experience what is to be looked for of a niggardly Demea, of a crafty Davus, of a flattering Gnatho, of a vainglorious Thraso; and not only to know what effects are to be expected, but to know who be such, by the signifying badge given them by the comedian.[70]

The White Queen's Pawn, like Sidney, expects an orderliness conspicuously absent from the playing of the Black House (and chess-play and stage-play are conflated in the ambiguous last line of her speech quoted above).

In the closing lines, all the tensions in the White Queen's Pawn's speech come to a head, with the mutation of the dominant metaphor. In most uses of the "world as a stage" trope, the audience is not usually involved: the focus is on the actors. But here, the "assembly," the "mighty auditory," is suddenly brought to the fore. It is no theological abstraction, nor is it equal to anything like "God and the angels," because she raises the possibility of religious conflict within the audience. It is expected to be predominantly Protestant, but possibly containing one or two Catholic sympathisers. In fact it is the audience of the theatre, suddenly aware of the artificiality of what they are watching. The Epilogue repeats this idea, even down to the word "assembly," but changes its effect; the speaker brings a message from the White Queen to those whose support for the White Queen has been their motive in coming,

> Which she hopes most of this assembly draws.
> For any else, by envy's mark denoted,
> To those night glow-worms in the bag devoted,
> Where'er they sit, stand, or in private lurk,
> They'll be soon known by their depraving work.
> (Epilogue 4-8)

He projects the divisions of the play outwards upon the audience. Rather than saying "the fiction has ended," the Epilogue perpetuates the fiction that the play is *not* a fiction. Whereas the play began with a distancing Induction—bracketing the whole play as a dream shown by Error to the damned soul of Ignatius Loyola—that bracket is never closed at the end of the play. Instead the Epilogue invites the audience to look at themselves, to hunt out Catholics sitting or standing among them. The Epilogue, in effect, casts audience members as pawns of the two Houses, inviting them to live up to their roles in an extra-theatrical reality: a logical extension of what the play itself had been doing with Gondomar, de Dominis, and the other living contemporaries satirised. Personation puts the borderline between stage and audience under great stress.

In short, *A Game at Chess* has a highly allegorical, non-realistic style of presentation, and yet the most sympathetic characters in it insist on strict standards of representational sobriety that are flouted by the fiction within which they participate. The resulting tensions could be anthropomorphised almost as a self-loathing. And one is now in a position to answer the question with which we started—whether *A Game at Chess* is presented as drama or as text. *A Game at Chess* presents dramatic imagery with a certain hostility: in attributing to the Black Bishop's Pawn the characteristics of a player in the clothes of a person he is not, it comes dangerously close to condemning itself. This suspicion of playing is part of the thematic, almost obsessive repetition of the word "play" with a wide range of associations, from sex to chess to drama. But on the other hand, the suspicion of drama can be linked to a suspicion of *all* textual production; a suspicion centred upon books and letters, but extending outward to include orations, poems, songs, and dances. So for Middleton, the distinction between text and performance is by no means as clear-cut as it had been for Jonson in *Poetaster*, or for Dekker in *Satiromastix*, or even as it was for Middleton's contemporary critics in the Privy Council. And in an apparent effort to stabilise the play's meanings, the drama's Prologue offers a vision of meaning determined by formalised, stylised chess rules, because only this can escape the radical indeterminacy of textuality—in Barthesian parlance, its "playfulness."

Finally, to what extent is all this Aristophanic? Swinburne is clearly right in general terms: the play's fantasy, metatheatricality, and patriotic satire do recall the comedy of Aristophanes. But most of all, in its representation of living contemporaries, it *is* part of what Renaissance observers saw as a revival of Old Comedy. For Swinburne is not the first writer to make a comparison between *A Game at Chess* and Greek Old Comedy; that honour goes to William Prynne, whose thousand-page denunciation of stage-plays, *Histriomastix*, came out in 1633. At one point he asserts that drama is evil because of its bitterness and its representation of real people in comedies. His survey starts with "that scurrilous carping *Comaedian*" Aristophanes, runs through Eupolis and stories of Roman satirical plays, and ends up with contemporary plays that attack real people. Among the victims he mentions are "Gundemore, the late Lord Admirall, Lord Treasurer, and others," very probably an allusion to *A Game at Chess*.[71]

Like the other professional comedies that have been discussed in this chapter, it combines this satirical personation with a strong and surprising interest in issues of textuality and theatricality. To reduce it to schematic terms, one may say that *The Whore of Babylon* is very pro-text, *The Roaring Girl* very pro-theatre, and *Swetnam* very anti-text; but *A Game at Chess* is anti-text and anti-theatre at the same time, and indeed starts to challenge the sharp dichotomy between the two so strongly maintained by the plays of the War of the Theatres. As is to be seen in the next chapter, it is a distinction which for Jonson too becomes more problematic in the years after the War.

CHAPTER FOUR

After the War: Jonson

Jonson's *Ode to Himself*, written on the occasion of the failure of *The New Inn*, attracted a number of replies by both detractors and admirers. Among the latter, one "I. C." sought to reassure the poet that his work was indeed worthwhile. He contrasted the discourtesy of modern audiences with the magnanimity that prevailed in ancient Athens, and in particular with Socrates' reaction to his satirical personation in *Clouds*:

> [Athens'] greatest Senators did silent sit,
>   Heare and applaud the wit,
> Which those more temperate Times,
> Us'd when it tax'd their Crimes:
> *Socrates* stood, and heard with true delight,
> All that the sharpe *Athenian* Muse could write
>
>   Against his suppos'd fault;
>   And did digest the salt
> That from that full vaine did so freely flow:
>   And though that we doe know
> The Graces joyntly strove to make that brest
>   A Temple for their rest,
>   We must not make thee lesse
> Than *Aristophanes*:
> He got the start of thee in time and place,
> But thou hast gain'd the Goale in Art and Grace.[1]

For I. C., as well as for several other contemporary eulogists, Jonson's literary credentials as a dramatic satirist were assured by this precedent. Aristophanes was a model for Jonson, and ought to guarantee liberty for dramatic satire aimed at reforming the audience. But to judge from Jonson's comments on *Clouds* in *Discoveries*, I. C.'s attempted compliment to him might verge on the tactless:

> What could have made them laugh, like to see *Socrates* presented, that Example of all good life, honesty, and vertue, to have him hoisted up with a Pullie, and there play the Philosopher, in a basquet? Measure, how many foote a Flea could skip *Geometrically*, by a just Scale, and edifie the people from the ingine? This was *Theatricall* wit, right Stage-jesting, and relishing a Play-house, invented for scorne, and laughter.[2]

Aristophanes the Athenian writer, guided by the Muse: Aristophanes the stage-jester. These are the two alternative views of personal satire and personation that are in conflict throughout the Jonson canon. With Jonson, more than any other writer of the period, the issue of personation is inescapably important, as every one of his major comedies has been dogged by allegations of personal satire.

One should begin with *Volpone* (1606): Jonson's first non-collaborative comedy after the War of the Theatres, and a play whose preface denies that Jonson has ever engaged in personation except of a "mimic, cheater, bawd or buffon" worthy to be satirised. This elegantly ambiguous phrase, of course, admits as much as it denies. For Jonson, indeed, personally satirical drama is the norm among his rivals who "care not whose liuing faces they intrench, with their petulant stiles." By contrast, *Volpone* deals in ideal types, in a Venice whose physical and ethical difference from London is harped upon within the play. However, as Robert C. Evans has shown, some early readers of *Volpone* saw it precisely as a specimen of the topical, personal drama that Jonson claimed to be repudiating.[3] Evans produces several seventeenth-century sources, including John Aubrey, who say that Volpone himself is a representation of Thomas Sutton, the wealthiest commoner in England, who like Volpone had many people lobbying to be his heir. At his eventual death in 1611 (five years after *Volpone* was staged), the money went to found the institution of Charterhouse. The language of Evans' witnesses, most of whom unfortunately are writing after the Restoration, suggests intentionality: "by Seigneur Volpone is meant Sutton"; "Ben: Johnsons *Vulponi* is generally reported to be master Sutton's humour"; "'Tis said that Ben Johnson in his Volpone: =personated, Master Sutton the founder of Suttons Hospitall." One of these writers even goes so far as to compare Jonson's personation with Aristophanes'.[4]

But biographically, there are major differences between Volpone and Sutton; most crucially, the issue of class. Volpone is a nobleman, as is frequently stressed in the play, whereas Sutton was a commoner, and this in itself is enough to scupper any exact identification between the two. But it is outside the scope of this project to speculate on the effects of this possible identification on one's perception of *Volpone*. What is interesting is that even a play which goes to great lengths to portray itself as part of a fictional, stylised, alien and distant world, was still seen by many early observers as part of a libelling, personating enterprise. Evans has caught a piece of Renaissance "application," which according to Jonson has "growne a trade with many" (*Volpone* Dedication 65). It seems to have been an activity to which Jonson's plays, above all others, were particularly susceptible.

In a similar vein, the prefatory material to *Epicoene* again explicitly denies that there is any personal satire in it: "*Poet* neuer credit gain'd / By writing truths, but things (like truths) well fain'd." Or as Beaumont put it in his commendatory poem, "he that strongly writes" an exposition of general vices is going to end up expressing "priuate faults" so well that the victims will be convinced it is directed personally against them. The play is thus armoured with denials of personal satire. But John Dryden, no less, recorded that he was "assured from divers persons that Ben Jonson was actually acquainted with such a man," and the story of Jonson's modelling of Morose on a particular victim is repeated independently elsewhere.[5]

Likewise, there are plenty of allegations of personal satire concerning *The Alchemist.* Jasper Mayne, in his elegy on Jonson, mentioned and half-denied assertions that Face and Sir Epicure Mammon were representations of real people. In 1668 Margaret Cavendish jokingly offered one reading of the characters: Jonson "expressed Kelly by Capt. Face, and Dee by Dr. Subtle, and their two Wives by Doll Common, and the Widow; by the Spaniard in the play, he meant the Spanish Ambassador, and by Sir Epicure Mammon, a Polish Lord."[6] Although Cavendish's episode is a satirical presentation of "application," it presupposes that such "application" happened. Another writer from the Restoration period to see personal application in the play was the anonymous compiler of a manuscript now in the Bodleian, who notes, "Ben: Johnson also is said to have deciphered in his Alchymist one Reynold an Apothecary."[7] I leave the full investigation of this connection to someone else, since once again all that matters for the topic under discussion is that—in spite of *The Alchemist*'s avowals to the contrary—the play was seen as an Aristophanic exercise in personation: a use of what Mayne called "th'old *Comick* freedome."

Jonson's next comedy, *Bartholomew Fair*, is similarly controversial. David McPherson has demonstrated the ways in which Adam Overdo's behaviour and language recall quite strikingly that of one Thomas Middleton (no relation to the dramatist), Lord Mayor of London, who was known to go round the city in disguise checking weights and measures as Overdo hopes to.[8] Nonetheless, any possibility of personal reference is complicated by the fact that—as McPherson also shows—this is at the same time an example of the literary device of the "disguised duke" common in tragicomedies of the period like *Measure for Measure* and Marston's *The Fawn*. In other words, life is imitating art as much as *vice versa*.

But a second connection between this play and personal satire concerns Lanthorne Leatherhead, the owner of the puppets, and Jonson's collaborator and rival Inigo Jones, whose privileging of theatrical effects in masques over their poetry could be seen as reflected in Leatherhead's puppetry. For instance, Jonson's friend John Selden in his *Table Talk*, referring to the puppets in the context of the futility about arguing over matters of faith, refers quite incidentally to the master of the puppets as "Inigo Lanthorne."[9] It was a comparison also made by Jonson himself, who likened Jones to Leatherhead in his *Expostulation with Inigo Jones*, an angry verse satire written in the 1630s. However, in this poem Jonson also likens Jones to Adam Overdo. Jones can't be both at once, at least not according to a useful definiton of personation, and the very fact that Jonson needs to draw attention to such possible connections implies that they were not self-evident at the original reception of the play. Further evidence against the *Bartholomew Fair* identification includes the facts that Jones and Jonson had hardly met in the period leading up to the writing of the play, as they were both travelling abroad, and that there is little evidence of a feud between them so early in their careers. It wasn't until Jonson's late and problematic play *A Tale of a Tub* that the conflict between himself and Jones over the nature of theatre, and the role of spectacle within it, spilt over into clear personation of Jones on the professional stage.

But it remains true that a connection between Jones and Leatherhead with his "Lanterne-lerry" was made by Jonson after the event. And Greek Old Comedy is referred to, not merely in echoes within *Bartholomew Fair*, but in the *Expostulation* itself. At one point in it Jonson says of Jones, "His name is Σκευοποιός wee all knowe, / The maker of ye Propertyes!"[10] *Skeuopoioi* are the mask-makers of Greek drama, whose most famous moment in classical literature is in Aristophanes' *Knights*, where the character representing Cleon is introduced, and Demus explains that his mask does not portray him to the life, as the *skeuopoioi* were too afraid of the consequences.[11] If Jones is the cowardly time-server unwilling to fulfil the intentions of the dramatist, then Jonson—of course—is casting himself as Aristophanes, and implicitly justifying his personal satire of Jones to boot.

Such "back-personation," as one might call it—assigning personal reference to a play one has written that may not have been present in it when composed—would not be without parallel. Another example, from the works of Philip Massinger, is discussed in the next chapter, and there again Aristophanes is invoked as a justification. So here Jonson is himself engaging in the sort of "application" of the play discouraged not merely, as we have seen, in the Dedication to *Volpone* but also in the Induction to *Bartholomew Fair* itself with its condemnation of the activities of the "politique *Picklocke* of the *Scene*" (Induction 138). This sort of self-inflicted application may go part of the way towards explaining why the Jonson canon is dogged with allegations of personation which do not seem to have stuck to the plays of Shakespeare in the same way.

Moving on to 1616, one may start with Jonson's own description of the next play he wrote:

> A play of his upon which he was accused the Divel is ane ass, according to Comedia Vetus, jn England the divell was brought jn either w' one Vice or other, the Play done the divel caried away the Vice, he brings jn ye divel so overcome w' ye wickednes of this age that <he> thought himself ane ass<.> παρεργως is discoursed of the Duke of Drown land. the King desyred him to conceal it.[12]

Yet again, the spectre of Aristophanes appears, since *Vetus Comedia*, although used here of the conventions of old English comedy, most naturally refers to the Greek drama. Indeed, there was a tendency in Renaissance literary criticism to conflate the two.[13] Jonson's combination of the two in this case is confirmed by internal evidence in the play itself: the Vice describes himself in a strange classicising phrase as "*vetus Iniquitas*" (*The Devil is an Ass*, Prologue 47). Old English Comedy is being perceived through the spectacles of a classicist. Not merely that, but quotations from Aristophanes in the original Greek even appear in the play, among the lines spoken by the feigningly possessed Fitzdotterel.[14] Moreover, one finds that the play as a whole is highly topical and possibly even a vehicle for personal satire. On this subject, there is a long and provocative study by Robert C. Evans.[15] Evans argues the case for the extreme topicality of references to the topics of monopolies, demonic possessions, a possible Spanish match, and to the business of reclaiming drowned land. In particular, he amasses evidence that personal reference to the Lord Chief Justice Edward Coke may be present in Sir Paul Either-Side. Such cases are easy to make and hard to prove, but Evans' case is cautious and convincing: convincing at the very least that *The Devil is an Ass* addresses issues that were not going to make the Lord Chief Justice particularly comfortable if he were among the audience.

In *The Staple of News* (1625), Jonson's direct imitation of Aristophanes and his frankness of personal satire both reach a peak. The Aristophanic imitation comes in the form of a range of borrowed elements: a dog-trial modelled extensively upon *Wasps*, verbal parallels with *Plutus* in a personification of Wealth (Lady Pecunia), and the device of the Staple itself, a fast-talking trickster's lair with strong echoes of the Phrontisterion in *Clouds*. As for the personal satire, it occurs in the character of Nathaniel, and to an extraordinary degree. In this entire period, only Joseph Swetnam and Moll Cutpurse are displayed as explicitly upon the comic stage, under their own names, as Nathaniel Butter, printer and newspaper pioneer, is displayed here.[16]

Nathaniel is a clerk in the Staple of News, an organisation that sells news itself as if it were a commodity. The Register names him within a few lines of his first appearance, passing a customer over to him; since she is a butter-woman, it is Nathaniel she must consult. The "butter" pun, strongly implying Nathaniel's surname, is one that will crop up over and over again. In particular, it is a favourite with the four Gossips. In the Intermean at the end of Act II, for instance, Expectation wishes the Staple to open, and adds: "would *Butter* would come in, and spread it-selfe a little to vs" (Intermean II, 51-52). The ensuing twenty lines contain the word "butter" no fewer than fourteen times, as the Gossips go into a series of excruciating jokes about the sort of butter they might expect. All of this is nonsensical unless Nathaniel is a representation of Nathaniel Butter.

Nathaniel reads news that comes in from the Westminster Emissary and it becomes clear that he is a subordinate clerk, though one with a certain amount of authority in the ordering of the Staple. He is described by Fitton and Cymbal, the masters of the operation:

CYMBAL: A decay'd Stationer
He was, but knowes *Newes* well, can sort and ranke 'hem.

FITTON: And for a need can make 'hem.

CYMBAL: True *Paules* bred,
I' the *Church-yard*. (I.v.120-23)

Biographically, this is an accurate if pejorative summary of the life of the real Nathaniel Butter, son of a printer, and himself a printer by trade before specialising in the writing and compiling of news-books. As for the idea of a monopoly of news, it is perhaps an imaginative extension of the events of late 1624, when a syndicate was set up to control all newsbook production in England.[17] In the surreal, Aristophanic context it would be irrelevant to ask for a naturalistic explanation of why

Nathaniel is a subordinate clerk in the new enterprise, whereas the historical Butter appears to have been head of the 1624 cartel.[18]

Nathaniel is on stage throughout III.ii, the long scene set in the Staple which is the centrepiece of the play. Of the various things he does during it, and the comments he interjects, the most interesting involves a switch in his job. At first, Nathaniel is responsible for Protestant news, while his partner Thom (whose place has been bought for him by the prodigal hero, Penny-Boy Junior) covers Catholic news. Penny-Boy Junior is dissatisfied with this arrangement, and by offering Nathaniel a sum of money induces him to swap jobs with Thom; clearly a point is being made about Nathaniel's venality, but I suggest below that there is more at stake in this exchange. This scene is the climax of the Staple plot, and after it Nathaniel is not heard of again until the news of the mysterious explosion of the Staple, at which point Thom describes his fate: "My Fellow melted into butter" (V.i.49). (Jonson does not content himself with imagining the punishment and reformation of his satirical victim, as in the War of the Theatres: nothing less than total liquefaction will suffice here.) Introduced as Butter and dissolved as Butter, Nathaniel is therefore a representation of Nathaniel Butter.

It is not surprising that Butter did not enjoy Jonson's caricature of him. Alexander Gill, another of Jonson's literary victims, imagines Butter alongside Inigo Jones, yet a third, all joining in mocking the poor reception of *The Magnetic Lady* in 1632:

> O how thy frind, *Natt Butter*, gan to Melte
> Whenas the poorenes of thy plott he smelte,
> And *Inigo* w'h laughter ther grewe fatt
> That thear was Nothing worth the Laughing att.[19]

Not for Butter, evidently, a graceful Socratic acceptance of his fate as butt of a stage caricature. It is tempting to take Gill's joke about Butter melting as a specific allusion to his fate on stage in *The Staple of News*, although—as the reference to Butter in *A Game at Chess* discussed above demonstrates—it was an obvious joke to make.

Indeed, *The Staple of News* comes close to *A Game at Chess* on numerous counts: notably in the way that they share an extraordinary frankness in their personally satirical attack. Something else that *The Staple* shares with Middleton's play is an atypical, un-Jonsonian distaste for textuality. Like the cabinet of intelligences in *A Game at Chess*, the Staple when opened is full of letters and documents—all unreliable and deceptive—that are displayed on stage and read aloud. The Staple offers a world where changing sides in the religious debate is as easy as it was for

Middleton's Fat Bishop: "It is but penning / Another recantation."
For when Thom changes from the Papal reporter to the Protestant reporter, swapping places with Nathaniel, " 'Tis but writing so much ouer
againe."[20]
The most spectacular expression of this disdain for text is an exchange which combines a Rabelais reference, a topical reference to the
rival play, and a sort of exceeding and consuming of that play:

> THOM: There is a *Legacy* left to the *Kings Players*,
> Both for their various shifting of their *Scene*,
> And dext'rous change o' their persons to all shapes,
> And all disguises: by the right reuerend
> *Archbishop* of *Spalato*.
>
> LICKFINGER: He is dead,
> That plai'd him!
>
> THOM: Then, h' has lost his share o' the *Legacy*.
>
> LICKFINGER: What newes of *Gundomar*?
>
> THOM: A second *Fistula*,
> Or an *excoriation* (at the least)
> For putting the poore *English-play*, was writ of him,
> To such a sordid vse, as (is said) he did,
> Of cleansing his *posterior's*.
>
> LICKFINGER: Iustice! Iustice!   (III.ii.201-12)

In the Middleton play, the Fat Bishop and the Black Knight (caricatures
of the "right reverend / *Archbishop*" and Gundomar) are of all the
characters the ones most associated with texts of all sorts. Jonson, like
Middleton, juxtaposes text and performance, imagining one victim
applauding the acting, the other maltreating the text. Sadly, Jonson's
wording does not reveal whether it was the newly-published quarto, or
one of the many manuscript versions in circulation, that so inflamed the
diplomat.[21]
Even outside the Staple scenes, many documents appear on stage
in the play. When first seen, Penny-Boy Junior is going through a
sheaf of bills; Picklock appears holding a legal document, a schedule;
Piedmantle brings in Pecunia's pedigree (I.i, I.vi.34, IV.iv). The stage-
direction specifies that there are papers on Penny-Boy Senior's desk at
the start of V.iv, and the whole plot of Act V with Picklock revolves
around two documents—a penitent letter and a legal deed. Again, a
good number of these documents are in some way trickeries: the deed,
and the bills, for instance. Furthermore, documents are made anthro-

107

pomorphic. Of Lady Pecunia's four attendants, Band, Wax, Statute and Mortgage, two are representations of sorts of documents, and the other two accessories to documents. Like *A Game at Chess* this is a play that revolves around bits of paper, and the bits of paper come out of it quite badly.

Texts, and by extension, the "cornucopiae"[22] of writings produced by the office are being mocked, but theatre is being given an unaccustomed power here. The joke about the legacy, for instance, depends upon the coincidence that both William Rowley (the actor who played De Dominis) and De Dominis himself have died within the last year. Personating theatre is credited with an alarmingly powerful imitative power, a sinister actorly mimesis, that extends beyond the ostensible bounds of the play. It is the obverse of the power of clothes discussed above in connection with *A Game at Chess*: now it is the owner who influences the wearer, and not *vice versa*. All of this is especially strange, and especially self-referential, when spoken on a stage already occupied by Nathaniel, who is himself a personation of a real individual.

Obviously, there is a link between the play's negative presentation of news, and its negative presentation of textuality in the form of items of news. What could be the motives behind such an attack on newsbooks in general and Butter in particular at this time? How might such satire fit into Jonson's larger pattern of thinking about drama, and into his political agenda? Sarah Pearl has suggested that the masques of this period of Jonson's career share a political stance, in which stress is laid upon the need to maintain the authority of the king, particularly in the area of Britain's position in relation to Europe. When it comes to the treatment of news in *News from the New World Discovered in the Moon*, *Neptune's Triumph* and *The Staple of News*, this stance manifests itself in a dislike of the news trade since it permitted unlicensed comment upon that foreign policy. More broadly, the news trade is also a rival to drama. Pearl suggests that in *The Staple of News*, "Jonson is declaring his dislike of fictionalised versions of current events."[23]

This idea can be taken further, and Jonson's objections need not just be macropolitical. For instance, 1625 saw the printing of *Paper's Complaint*, in which Paper objects to the vast increase in the production of poor-quality text that it is forced to bear.[24] Among the genres singled out for attention are playtexts,

> Where each man *in*, and out *of's humour* pries,
> Upon himselfe: and laughs vntill he cries.
> *Untrussing humerous Poets*, and such *Stuffe* . . .   (141-43)

For "*Apollos* Priests" to have sunk so low as to have written and published personally satrical plays is both a shame to them and an abuse of the great potential of poetry. Also condemned are ballads, pornography, and the use of paper as toilet paper, a prospect concerning which Paper is especially unhappy. The continuation by Abraham Holland adds to the list satires against Spain and complains about the relative neglect of the poetry of Jonson, Drayton and other serious authors. (*A Game at Chess* could certainly be categorised as a satire against Spain, and in this play Jonson recategorises it as toilet paper as well.) The climax of the poem is an attack on newsbooks, with their fanciful stories of Bethlem Gabor and others, which cover reams of paper with such nonsense, while "Th' Impostors that these *Trumperies* doe vtter, / Are, A, B, C, D, E, F, G, and (- - - - -)" (Continuation 136-37,151-52).

So in 1625—the year of *The Staple*—Jonson and Butter are both under attack for the same sort of profligate waste of paper. Jonson is praised for his poetry, but his plays are criticised, and classed with newsbooks. In response to this sort of pressure, I suggest, Jonson's play responds by attacking Nathaniel Butter in particular and through him newsbooks in general, defining itself oppositionally as something more worthy, and abandoning for this purpose the normal Jonsonian privileging of textuality. (The Jonson of, say, *Poetaster* would not have been described as having "torne the booke [i.e. the prompt-book] in a *Poeticall* fury" just before the performance.) The one direct mention of playbooks is defensively classicising, an oblique assertion of their intellectual and literary merit: Jonson has the ignorant Gossip Censure complain about the education of children, "wee send them to learne their *Grammar*, and their *Terence*, and they learn their play-books" (Intermean III, 48-49). The issue at stake in *The Staple of News* is not just newsbooks, but whether newsbooks are of equal textual and literary status with plays and playbooks.

Yet again, the wider poetical implications of the play turn out to dovetail with a "micropolitical" motive for the personal representation and ridicule of Nathaniel Butter on stage. As has been seen, in all of Jonson's plays the possibility, or even the threat, of personal satire is not a negligible factor. But in *The Staple of News* it becomes, once more, completely central. It is no surprise, then, that it coincides with the most extensive imitations of Aristophanes in any Jonson play, which function not merely as devices in their own right, but as assertions that personal satire has an unimpeachable and highly literary pedigree.

Jonson's last plays abandon neither Aristophanic reference nor Aristophanic practice. In *The Magnetic Lady* he continues to model passages on Aristophanes in a device once again recalling the Aristophanic parabasis.[25] In *A Tale of A Tub* he represents Inigo Jones on the stage with undiminished vigour, again in the context of a row about the theory and practice of drama. And not merely did he continue to use personation as a weapon: as the next chapter shows, he continued to be a victim of it.

CHAPTER FIVE

The Second War of the Theatres

This chapter traces how arguments about the nature and future of good theatre continue to be connected with personation and personal satire in plays through the 1630s. The debate is still about the status of professional drama, but is now given a special class dimension by the animus between professional playwrights such as Richard Brome and Philip Massinger, and court dramatists such as John Suckling and William Davenant. Yet again, personation is not simply a way of venting spleen against one's enemies, but a way of attacking their definition of comic drama: in this case, linked, furthermore, to practical struggles over ownership and control of playhouses, in which struggles these texts may be seen as interventions.

The theatre of the 1630s as a whole has suffered from relative neglect when compared to the interest in the theatre of earlier decades. What criticism there is has often been vitiated by anachronistic anticipation of the coming Civil War. It has been assumed by some critics that Brome, Davenant and the rest could see the Civil War coming, and the works of these writers have been read accordingly as nostalgic, fatalistic, and even elegiac. In fact, as has been pointed out by Martin Butler, the writers of the time were gifted with no such anticipatory hindsight.[1] They didn't expect that the theatres would be closed in 1642, and they were not writing a full stop to the dramatic history of their time. As a result of such re-evaluation, there is a body of good recent work on these "late" playwrights, on which I draw in what follows; and the drama itself is coming to be seen as just as inventive, vital, and engaged as what went before.

There is an important dividing-line in this drama, which like most such dividing-lines blurs under close scrutiny. But broadly speaking, one can divide the playwrights of the professional stage—the Jonsons and Dekkers and their colleagues—from a new breed of fundamentally amateur courtier playwrights, who wrote for the professional theatre not for the sake of earning money but as a literary endeavour, inspired by the very success of the earlier professional writers who had tried to give the theatre literary respectability.[2]

During the 1630s, it became fashionable for courtiers to write plays for the professional theatre companies. One is not concerned here about plays such as Montague's *Shepherd's Paradise*, written and performed by courtiers, but about plays such as Sir John Suckling's *Aglaura*, which was performed (1637/8) at a public theatre, although using scenery from court masques. Acted by professional troupes at their normal venues, these plays attracted audiences away from the more regular entertainments written by full-time writers and offered, according to Ira Clark, "a genuine economic and a perceived aesthetic threat" to the professional playwrights.[3] As a matter of fact, the antithesis is less clear-cut than Clark's phrase suggests. The economic conditions dictated and were reinforced by the poetics of spectacle, in the same way that the conditions of censorship dictated and were reinforced by the poetics of satire: to separate the poetics from the economics is like asking what Homer would have *really* written if he hadn't been tied down to a tedious hexameter metre and a style derived from oral composition.[4]

Let us consider the economic threat. The court writers might have been less skilful at the construction of plays than their professional counterparts, but they had two key advantages, of which the more important was spectacle. The public performance of *Aglaura* in 1637/8 had not merely court masque scenery, but costumes provided by Suckling at a cost to him of three or four hundred pounds.[5] Such spectacle was completely outside the budgets of those who produced plays as a paying proposition. The second reason for the success of such plays was more subtle. They were, as Martin Garrett points out, simply more fashionable than the professional drama, being associated with aristocrats and aristocratic money, and being occasions to be seen as much as to see.[6]

Nevertheless, the true extent of the economic damage to the companies, and to the playwrights, from these courtier-authored plays remains difficult to assess. Sharpe and Butler both suggest that it was fairly slight to the companies; for instance, professional companies were still coming to play at the court itself, and they were acting the plays provided by the amateurs. Nonetheless, to the professional writers, the threat must have been far worse. Courtier plays were given for free, or even (according to Brome in *The Court Begger*) given with a sum of money, like vanity publishing.

A further complication in attempting to quantify this change in the nature of dramatic writing is that with many of the writers, one cannot tell whether or not their plays were written with the objective of earning a living. In the absence of playhouse accounts, it can't even be said how many of the plays were given for free or handed over along with a subvention. However, one can see from G. E. Bentley's list of 170 plays known to have been performed by the King's Men between 1616 and 1642, that many well-known courtier figures contributed to their repertoire, almost all during the reign of Charles. The plays by courtly writers such as Lodowick Carlell, William Berkeley, William Cartwright, William Cavendish, Sir John Denham, William Habington, Thomas Killigrew, Henry Killigrew and Sir John Suckling, would to some extent reduce the King's Men's dependence upon and market for full-time professionals.[7]

One figure who further complicates the picture is William Davenant, who can be connected in one way or another to most of the theatrical disputes of the 1630s, including the texts that will be under discussion here. Again, Davenant's own personal finances are not available for inspection, but he appears to have earned money from playwriting even while associating with courtly writers and while decrying the barbaric state of the public theatre in a way that marks him out as distinct from his professional brethren such as Brome, Shirley, Massinger and Ford. An example that illustrates these conflicts is the case of his play *The Just Italian*, a tragicomedy, licensed on 2 October 1629 and performed at the Blackfriars not long after.[8] In the circumstances and texts surrounding this play, one may see the first developments in the "second war of the theatres."

The Just Italian provoked a minor furore, but not on its appearance on stage, where by all accounts it was something of a failure. The furore was a result of its publication in quarto in 1630, along with commendatory verses by the courtier Thomas Carew. Carew blamed the failure of the play on the low quality of the audience: they were an "untun'd Kennel," "crowded heaps" of undiscriminating auditors who did not appreciate real poetry. Philip Massinger rose to Carew's bait in a Prologue presented before his tragi-comedy *The Maid of Honour* in 1630—the same year the offending verses were printed. Massinger's Prologue, like the other two poems associated with it here, was only discovered in 1980, and it provides important new evidence on the extent of the "second war." Massinger derides "such as would seeme Critiques of the age," and verbal echoes leave no doubt that his target is Carew and his verses on *The Just Italian*.[9]

This Prologue in turn attracted a manuscript satire against Massinger, addressed "To my honored ffriend," that is, to Carew himself. The anonymous author takes Carew's part in dispraising the vulgarity of the popular theatre, and states the division between Carew the courtier and Massinger the professional playwright with devastating simplicity: "yo" for pleasure sing, he sweats for food."[10] The author of this third entry in the quarrel may well be William Davenant himself, the failure of whose play originally sparked it off. Such an identification, first made by Peter Beal, has been adopted with enthusiasm by recent writers on Massinger such as Martin Garrett.[11]

A copy of "To my honored ffriend" evidently made its way to Massinger, for he responded in another manuscript satire, in angry, pell-mell couplets. He justifies his profession by reference to "Clasique Poets" who earned money from drama, Terence and Statius. He derides his attacker, firstly for remaining anonymous, secondly for having himself gained money from theatrical writing—another suggestion that Davenant may be the person under attack. And as for the offending Prologue itself, he justifies that early on by reference to Aristophanes:

> Yo" mett a coppie of my Prologue, true;
> 'Twas therefore writt. Why did it nettle yo",
> Beinge Aim'de at an other? 'Twas my end
> To haue it vnderstood. Yo' honored freind
> hear[d] it vpon ye stage with confidence
> Like another Socrates, while yo' patience
> was forefeited in yo' Chamber to reade that
> In wch yo" found his reuerence pointed at.
>
>   ("A Charme for a Libeller" 35-42)

Massinger, like Jonson before him, invokes the example of *The Clouds* to justify his own personal satire. In 1630 arguments about the theory of professional theatre once again spill over very easily into personal abuse, perhaps even personal representation on stage.

One thing that does become clear from considering *The Maid of Honour* in connection with this theatrical dispute is that in the manuscript satire, Massinger *has* got his own play in mind. He is creating what one might call a back-personation of his anonymous opponent: he's figuring him as a character from *The Maid of Honour*. The character—or rather characters—in question are Anthonio and Gasparo, who make brief appearances only in the first three acts of this tragi-comedy about a woman who finally chooses to renounce the world's vanities. They are effeminate courtiers who try to take part in a military campaign and are defeated and humiliated. Massinger, pretending to be ignorant of his opponent's identity, is nonetheless quite specific about many of his

114

attributes, and they are attributes taken from these two minor characters in his own play.

The general resemblance is that Gasparo, Anthonio and the Libeller are all flatterers and cowards. More specifically, the Libeller wears "yor scarlet and yor plushe," and the courtiers wear "your skarlets, and your plush." Both are said to like prostitution and taverns.[12] Their victor Gonzago says they are too despicable to be worth arguing with: "I wrong my selfe / In parling with you"; Massinger says of his opponent, "yo" are not worth / A satire, or my Gall." For the courtiers both in the play and the poem, the best cure is to be beaten with a cudgel.[13]

Recognition of this back-personation affects one's appreciation of Massinger's satire. He is figuring the detractor of the play as its victim even in the act of detraction; and in seeking, even after the event, to introduce personal reference into his comedy, he is exercising the Aristophanic privilege he claimed for himself earlier in the poem. One is reminded of Jonson's similar claiming of Aristophanic privilege to assert after the event that personal satire against Inigo Jones had existed within *Bartholomew Fair*. As early as 1630, then, a new row about the status of theatre was being conducted in a series of texts that answered each other with escalating hostility and specificity. Furthermore, the row was threatening to boil over into personation, as it eventually did some years later in the works of Suckling and Brome.

After these hostilities, friction continued between those making a living by writing plays and those who treated it as a literary exercise. Davenant's own involvement was temporarily curtailed by the terrible attack of syphilis in 1630 that nearly killed him and cost him his nose. It wasn't until 1634 that he recovered sufficiently to mount his next play, whose failure once again he put down to faction and the "harsh Multitude."[14] But even with Davenant sidelined, the argument rumbled on. Further shots in the "untun'd kennell" row have been detected in the works of Thomas Heywood, William Habington, James Shirley, Thomas Randolph, and even years after the event in the verses of one Richard West.[15] This is a relatively new area in criticism, and it would not be surprising if new evidence of personations cropped up in plays of this period too. For instance, James Shirley, who is known to have contributed verse to the "untun'd kennell" row, ran into trouble with the Master of the Revels in 1632, with his play *The Ball*. Who were the "divers personated so naturally, both of lords and of others of the court" that made the Master of the Revels refuse it a licence until he was assured by the theatrical manager Beeston that the offending parts had been removed?[16]

Similar battle-lines are drawn up at about the same date in the prefatory verses to Richard Brome's *The Northern Lasse*, published in quarto in 1632, and featuring commendations from Ben Jonson and Thomas Dekker among others. Thirty years after attacking each other's drama in the War of the Theatres, Jonson and Dekker find themselves united in their praise of Brome. Jonson's contribution, indeed, offers a synthesis of his own insistence on comic laws and literary form with Dekker's insistence on the acid test of successful performance. According to Jonson, Brome receives

> Good applause,
> Which you have justly gained from the Stage,
> By observation of those Comick Lawes
> Which I, your *Master*, first did teach the Age.[17]

The failure of *The New Inn* in 1628/9 had not found Jonson so sanguine about the relationship between good comic laws and good stage reception, but here at least Jonson is in a bullish mood. Dekker, meanwhile, rather cheekily uses an expression more associated with Jonson, praising "my Sonne Broom" for the excellency of his plays. But what binds together Jonson and Dekker—along with John Ford in his accompanying verses, and a fourth contributor—is an attack on amateurs. Jonson mocks the "Court-Hobby-horse" who is attempting to write plays, while Dekker attacks "Pyed Ideots" who are trying to do the same. Jonson and Dekker are now united against a new threat to their drama, a new antithesis to face their synthesis. In some ways, the fact that writing drama for the players is now respectable enough to be a desirable courtly accomplishment represents a victory for Jonson's ideas of drama as literature. Unluckily, and perhaps unsurprisingly, many of the courtly dramatists had a particular dislike for the ex-bricklayer, and saw fit to define their own ideals of drama by personally insulting him.

Brome's enemy, Sir John Suckling, for instance, attacked Jonson in several plays and poems written in the 1630s. His unfinished and unacted tragedy *The Sad One* includes a minor character called Multecarni ("Much-flesh"), a vulgar poet and playwright who inhabits the Mermaid tavern, and bears more than a passing resemblance to the ageing Jonson.[18] Jonson again is under attack in "The Wits," a narrative poem written by Suckling in 1637 about the laureateship, and circulated in manuscript. Interestingly, this poem, which surveys more than 25 living writers with a claim to the laureateship, includes Davenant, Suckling himself, and Walter Montague, but ignores professional playwrights such as Brome, Shirley, Massinger, and Ford. *The Goblins*, a tragicomedy written by Suckling after 1637 and acted at the Blackfriars, contains another drunken poet fond of mythological masques, who is kidnapped and deluded into believing he is in hell. This too seems to be a personation of Jonson, shortly after Jonson's death.[19]

Suckling also staged *Aglaura* in 1637/8, using lavish costumes that he paid for himself, and then had it printed at his own expense. Brome, for whom as a professional writer neither of these extravagances was possible or desirable, responded in a manuscript satire that conflated and scorned them both together: "She that in *Persian* habits, made great brags, / Degenerates in this excess of rags."[20] But it is in 1639 and 1640 that the designs of Suckling and Davenant become most ambitious, and the friction with Brome and his ilk is at its worst. Then the "second war of the theatres" comes close to its parent, in terms of frankness of representation and directness of argument about theatre. In particular, the evidence for this is to be seen in Brome's play *The Court Begger*.

The Court Begger

The Court Begger (acted in 1640) is a departure from Richard Brome's normal technique, because it represents living contemporaries on stage, in the context of a row about the future of professional drama; and Brome is harking back to the first War of the Theatres in his strategies of representation. The living contemporaries in question are Sir William Davenant, and, even more conspicuously, Sir John Suckling. There is an elegant and thorough demonstration by R. J. Kaufmann that Ferdinando, the mad poetry-writing courtier, is a representation of Suckling.[21] Kaufmann shows how specific are the references to cribbage, the "hundred horse," and participation in military action against the Scots; in addition,

> Suckling was distinguished in a relatively small court circle as an aspiring soldier, as a successful, compulsive gambler, as a spectacular ladies' man, as an ambitious and successful favorite without accomplishment to justify his advancement, as a love poet, and as a notable coward. These are exactly the qualities Brome ascribes to Ferdinando. When we add that the two most discreditable episodes in Suckling's life — his refusal to fight a duel when beaten like a lackey and his flight at Berwick — are duplicated recognizably in the play, the probability of Sir Ferdinando being Suckling is made virtually certain.[22]

Kaufmann also identifies the ineffectual Court-Wit as a representation of William Davenant; particularly in respect of his dramatic ambitions, his masque-writing, and his deficiency of nose. These then are fairly savage and unmistakable representations of two prominent court figures.

117

One immediate reason for this uncharacteristic satirical representation turns out to be a battle about the control of playhouses. In 1639, Davenant and Suckling were engaged in a plan to build a new theatre in Fleet Street. On the evidence of the royal patent which they were granted, their theatre was to be unprecedentedly large—perhaps as much as forty yards square—and adapted for "Action, musical Presentments, Scenes, Dancing and the like," a far wider range of activities than for a normal playhouse.[23] This scheme fell through. Freehafer suggests the opposition of Sir Henry Herbert was a crucial factor, in which case Herbert would be fulfilling the role suggested for him by Richard Dutton as a sort of referee, assuring protection as well as regulation for the existing acting companies.[24] But balked, for whatever reason, of a theatre of his own, Davenant appears to have gone looking for an existing theatrical concern that he could take over; and the Cockpit Theatre, managed by the veteran William Beeston, with Richard Brome as its writer, seemed to be a tempting target. In fact, *The Court Begger* was being performed while the ownership of the theatrical company involved was itself in question.

Given that this is the context, I believe that *The Court Begger* is a play about the poetics and politics of professional theatre, in particular, about problems of monopolies. Brome's strategy is to link the predatory activities of Suckling and Davenant to a wider attack on monopolies, preferments, and courtly attitudes to private property.

One should start with the Prologue, which polarises current drama into two sorts. There is the "a new strayne of wit" that is gaining popularity among audiences, heavily reliant upon devices such as scene-painting, and on the other hand there is the type represented by Brome, "the Poet full of age and care," as he calls himself, who models his work upon "our great Masters of the Stage and Wit":

> Yet you to him your favour may expresse
> As well as unto those whose forwardnesse
> Make's them your Creatures thought, who in a way
> To purchace fame give money with their Play,
> Yet you sometimes pay deare for't, since they write
> Lesse for your pleasure than their own delight.
> Which if our Poet fayle in, may he be
> A Sceane of Mirth in their next Comedye.[25]

The last couplet here is, amongst other things, throwing down an open challenge to Suckling and Davenant. By inviting a riposte in kind, it tacitly admits that there is personal reference intended in this play against the enemy playwrights. In fact, it's an attempt to open a dialogue in plays, a War of the Theatres on the old model: a genre in which Brome clearly fancies his chances.[26] The idea that there is intertextual engagement going on is also suggested by the way the Suckling-character is introduced—in captivity and deluded. He wakes up, "bound and hooded, &c.," starts to write poetry, and erroneously concludes that he is in hell (220-21). This sardonic echo of how Suckling himself had introduced the Jonson-character in *The Goblins* (see above) serves further to link *The Court Begger* to an oppositional, almost dialectical model of drama.

Having noted the existence of the personal satire, one should now consider presentation of theatre within the play, before making the connections between the two topics. In the first act of *The Court Begger*, three projectors are introduced in turn, and each describes to the monopoly-obsessed court begger of the title, Sir Andrew Mendicant, a project that may make his fortune. The middle one is this:

> A new project
> For buylding a new Theatre or Play-house
> Upon the *Thames* on Barges or flat boats
> To helpe the watermen out of the losse
> They've suffer'd by Sedans; under which project
> The subject groanes, when for the ease of one
> Two abler men must suffer; and not the price,
> Or pride of Horse-flesh or Coach-hire abated.
> This shall bring flouds of gaine to th' watermen
> Of which they'l give a fourth of every fare
> They shall boord at the floating Theatre,
> Or set ashore from thence, the Poets and Actors
> Halfe of their first yeares profits. (194)

In other words, this plan—which Freehafer has shown to be a reference to Davenant and Suckling's Fleet Street project, complete with pun on "fleet"/"flat"—is presented as a monopoly, not as a straightforward business venture (thus misrepresenting the nature of the Fleet Street scheme). The reference to sedan-chairs makes this particularly pointed: there had indeed been a monopoly on this new method of travel, instituted in 1634 and already mocked by Brome.[27] A monopoly designed to alleviate other monopolies is absurd, and the effect is to link the sedan-chair monopoly, conceived of as a contribution to the class war, with the theatre plan as if that too had a similarly exclusive set of beneficiaries.

Furthermore, since this patent is the second of three discussed at length (as well as various briefer ideas for ingenious pretexts to tax people) one can get a better idea of its context by comparing it with the other two. The first is a monopoly in obtaining wigs from other people's hair, the third a monopoly whereby citizens pay to be assured that courtiers will not meddle with their wives. These monopolies are about using the court system to make money out of things that one does not own and has not nurtured—other people's hair, other people's marriages. The proposed floating theatre is literally and metaphorically without foundations.

A second monopoly to do with the theatre is proposed by Court-Wit (the Davenant-character) some scenes later:

> COURT-WIT: Sir, my affection leanes much to Poetry, especialy the *Drammatick*.
>
> SIR ANDREW MENDICANT: Writing of strange Playes?
>
> COURT-WIT: I am glad I speake sir, to your understanding. And my project is that no Playes may be admitted to the Stage, but of their making who Professe or indeavour to live by the quality: That no Courtiers, Divines, Students at Law, Lawyers-clearks, Tradesmen or Prentises be allow'd to write 'em, nor the Works of any lay-Poet whatsoever to be receav'd to the Stage, though freely given unto the Actors, nay though any such Poet should give a summe of money with his Play, as with an Apprentice, unlesse the Author doe also become bound that it shall doe true and faithfull service for a whole Terme.   (214-15)

Freehafer has taken this to be a statement of Brome's own position, that playwriting is a craft or art not to be dabbled in by amateurs, but that's not quite right, since, like the monopolistic floating theatre, this also is another attempt to buy drama. Court-Wit's idea is already contradicted, since he himself, a courtier, is blithely writing plays anyway. Court-Wit's apparent selflessness here is only as genuine as Swain-Wit's selflessness when he offers, a few lines later, to be hired to sleep with any handsome woman who is having difficulty conceiving a child.

What Court-Wit wants, in fact, is a monopoly, and this is made clearer by the second part of his scheme:

> I have another sir, to procure a Patent for my selfe to have the onely priviledge to give instructions to all the actors in the City, (especially the younger sort) the better to enable them to speake their parts emphatically and to the life.   (215)

120

This is a scheme which reflects Davenant's contemporary attempts to obtain possession of a company in London, and it is taken up again in the Epilogue. On this point, too, it seems to me that Freehafer has the emphasis wrong. His view is that the focus of *The Court Begger* is opposition to the Fleet Street project, and that the takeover of the Cockpit by Davenant, which did eventually take place, was something of an afterthought by the authorities. But in this play the Fleet Street theatre is relegated to being an anonymous projector's pipe-dream, unconnected with the schemes envisaged by Court-Wit himself. Surely, the whole play—and not just the Epilogue, as Freehafer suggests—is written with the threat of a takeover very much in mind.

In particular, the issue of class is linked to the theatre. The courtiers make various attempts to distance themselves from the sort of lower-class people that attend public playhouses, the "ill company" that Court-Wit dislikes, and their assumptions are one by one deflated. They blame the vulgar mob for thefts they have suffered at the playhouse, when it turns out that the thefts have been committed by one of their own number, Mr. Dainty (212). Lady Strangelove, whose accommodating nature permits all the courtiers to coexist in one circle, would like to introduce players to it too, and the blunt and admirable Swain-wit approves (246, 247, 211-12).

The satire of courtly dramatic practice is strongest in the inset entertainment in Act V, where Lady Strangelove's circle get together to create a masque to celebrate Charissa's wedding. It is written by Court-Wit, with choreography by the nimble but larcenous Mr. Dainty. On one level, the masque seems quite impressive, offering a pageant of Champions of the Queen of Love, acted by five of the courtiers:

> *Courage*, sent from *Mars*; *The Muses' skill*
> From wise *Apollo*. And the God, which still
> Inspires with subtilty, sly *Mercury*
> Sends this his *Agent*. Here's *Activity*
> From Jupiter himselfe; And from her store
> Of Spies, the Moon sends *This* to keepe the dore.[28]

These five roles are to be represented by Swain-Wit, Court-Wit, Dainty, Cit-Wit and the Doctor respectively, all of whom do indeed contain in some measure the allegorical quality they represent. But this impressive courtly allegorisation has been undermined in two ways. Firstly, we have been shown the work in preparation, the writer "scratching his head, as pumping his Muse," while people are awkwardly learning the dance steps and the Doctor sings false notes in the rehearsal. Even the boy

121

introducing the masque fluffs his lines (261, 259, 265). We have been permitted a view of the work under construction which offers us the chance to deconstruct it.

Secondly, we can see what a wretched compromise this masque is. The writer of this celebration of sexual love is Court-Wit, who is himself described as "pepper'd so full o' the whatsha callums, that his spittle would poyson a Dog or a Rat" (252), and who has in fact lost his nose through syphilis (this is a common theme in anti-Davenant satire). The heroic status of the five "heroes" he brings together is dubious at best. Swain-Wit has mocked Court-Wit's venereal disease to his face, and called Cit-wit's mother a whore, and has taken part in a feigned castration of the Doctor which has caused that character to lose control of his bowels in fear. Dainty, meanwhile, is a thief who has stolen both Swain-Wit's purse and Cit-Wit's woman, and been threatened with hanging. The Doctor has tried to abet a rape. And the role of the Queen of Love, whose champions they are, is to be played by Philomela the serving-woman whose own experiences of love have left her with nothing but an illegitimate child and, significantly, a dose of venereal disease. There is no need to suspect a causal relationship between Court-Wit's clap and Philomela's clap, or her illegitimate child, but the parallel does serve to make another point about the way that courtly irresponsibility is divorced from long-term consequences. A final twist which later becomes apparent is that the page-boy playing Cupid who speaks the introduction quoted above is the very child in question. In short, the monolithic front of the masque is contrasted with the sordid reality which it allegorises.

Indeed, the masque does not have the redemptive, curative force normally associated with Brome's inset dramas, notably in the central conceit of *The Antipodes*. The cures and reformations in this play are accomplished for the most part by threat of physical harm. The Doctor, Ferdinando, and Dainty confess their guilty secrets only when believing themselves to be on the point of being respectively castrated, stabbed, and challenged to a duel. Only Sir Andrew's conversion, brought about by a dance in which he is stripped of his chosen costume of papers and patents, is not of this violent sort. At the end of the play he renounces the fruitless search for monopolies and reversions, and the play ends with general rejoicing. But in many ways it carries a sting in its tail, in the form of its extraordinary Epilogue.

Received wisdom says the Epilogue was added by Brome later, once the previously unforeseen threat of a takeover became apparent, but I believe that it is an organic part of the play—indeed, the moment towards which the rest of the play has been building. It includes speeches delivered to the audience by no fewer than six of the play's characters, while the rest stand mutely by, giving it an unusual, and perhaps unique, choric dimension. Moreover, it returns to the theme of monopolies, and dramatic monopolies.

Swain-Wit begins by saying there is no need to apologise for the quality of the play to the "Audients." He will speak for all the characters, "and yet not beg for the Poet tho', why should we? has not he money for his doings? and the best price too? because we would ha' the best." He contrasts the author with those "great and curious Poets" who give money with their play: they beg for applause, but this poet has no need to beg for it (271). Swain-Wit leaps abruptly from arguing for the superiority of this dramatist over his amateur rivals, to a warning: William Beeston, the trainer of poets and players alike, is under threat from "the venemous practise of some, who study nothing more then his destruction." This direct reference to attempts to take over Beeston's company, we may now see, fits in thematically with the rest of the play. The description of Beeston as having "directed Poets to write and Players to speak till he traind up these youths here to what they are now" (272) significantly repeats the terms of the monopoly over choosing writers and teaching actors that Court-Wit sought earlier in the play itself. Thus the Epilogue is a thematic extension of the anti-monopoly satire of the play.

And this too is the thematic importance of Swain-Wit's allegations in the Epilogue that some courtly plays do not even belong to their purported authors, but are ghostwritten by scholars.[29] Like monopolists, the court dramatists get things made for them by other people and claim "'Tis mine": a practice which Brome links to their campaign to dispossess Beeston of his theatrical company. Brome, on the other hand, is arguing that there should be a free market in dramatic commerce. Allegations of plagiarism and ownership are at the heart of the justification of this act of personation just as they were forty years earlier for Jonson and Dekker. This reading also indicates the importance once again of the anti-Davenant motif of venereal disease, picked up in the Epilogue in puns such as this description of Brome: "Hee's no dandling on a Courtly lap, / Yet may obtaine a smile, if not a clap" (270)—so it recalls the poetic *and* personal failings of the enemies of Brome.

The Court Begger is therefore drama that attempts to alter a particular situation in the real world, namely the threat to Beeston's company. In its vision of the playhouse as a respectable place being given a bad reputation by larcenous courtiers, in its view of writing as a profession not a hobby, in the insistence of the Epilogue that theatre *is* a clear-eyed business transaction rather than requiring justification through special pleading, and in its bitter representation of living courtiers, it is as much an argument about poetics as personalities.

Whatever the effect produced upon the hearts and minds of its intended audience, *The Court Begger* did not amuse the authorities. It can probably be identified with the unlicensed play whose performance at the Cockpit was used as a pretext to have Beeston sacked and replaced with none other than William Davenant—the very outcome that the play is warning against.[30] If Davenant or Suckling were also contemplating an answer in dramatic form, events overtook them. In 1641 they were both implicated in the Army Plot to rescue the Earl of Strafford by force, and fled for their lives to France. Suckling made it to Paris, where, desperate and friendless, he committed suicide by poison within a few months.[31] Davenant—instantly recognisable thanks to his widely-publicised missing nose—was captured in England but survived to dominate early Restoration theatre and fashion it as he liked. It is remarkable that the works of Brome were almost entirely excluded from the Restoration stage.[32]

The old myth of an unproblematically Royalist "cavalier" drama set against a middle-class dramatic opposition has long been exposed as an oversimplification and an injustice to those covered by both labels. But within the sphere of poetics, I suggest, the "second war of the theatres" continues to be a valid term. One may summarize it as a series of verbal skirmishes between those who believed that drama was a species of literary activity, and those who thought that it required no such apology, since it was defined by what happened inside the playhouse in negotiation with the audience. Moreover, these verbal skirmishes sometimes developed into representation of one's theatrical enemies in stage comedies, an effect which seems to be a distinctive feature of disagreements about the status of professional drama in this period. Awareness of the existence of this "second war of the theatres," and the theoretical clashes it encapsulates, may well sharpen one's perception of the historical contexts of the works involved. One may conclude that Brome and Suckling, for instance, are not just writing plays that embody different political and social attitudes: they are writing entirely different species of plays, motivated by different poetics and interacting with theatrical conventions, expectations, and personnel in entirely different ways. They are not just saying different things: they are using different languages.

CONCLUSION

Satirical personation *did* happen on the English stage, and it mattered. To the plays featured in this study, it was central. For these plays, personation is not—as it has generally been considered—something introduced at the last minute as a private joke for those in the know. That sort of personation may well also have happened, it is true, but the sort displayed here is different: it shapes the plays in which it occurs and forms part of their wider context. Furthermore, other examples of this extensive personation, though lost to us, are certain to have existed, Chapman's *Old Joiner* being merely the best-documented. More personal reference may still be entirely undetected, and many existing allegations—especially concerning the plays of Jonson—remain not yet evaluated, and not yet linked to the wider concerns of the plays in which they occur; so work remains to be done in this field. However, what can be said is that most of the personally satirical comedies that survive are engaged in Wars of the Theatres of one sort or another. In the light of the foregoing discussion, one is now in a position to outline some of the common features that make these comedies into a distinct genre, and to summarise its progress through the period covered by this study.

Personally satirical comedies—at least, the ones that survive and are discussed here—are generally organised around depicting the reformation, or in a few cases, the destruction, of those they personate. Complimentary personation is rare, although it does exist; notably in *The Whore of Babylon, The Roaring Girl,* and the lost play of Turnholt. Many of the victims of personally satirical plays are playwrights who are rivals to the author; or, like Jonson's victims Charles Chester, Inigo Jones, and Nathaniel Butter, they are exponents of a form that is a rival in some way to professional drama. Among other victims, some are connected with the "woman question," including Moll Frith and Joseph Swetnam, and the effect of these personations is to destabilise formal paradigms of gender stereotypes. Still others are figures connected with religious controversy, and these are the ones (in *The Whore of Babylon* and *A Game at Chess*) who tend to be destroyed rather than reformed.

Another element that almost all those satirically personated have in common is that they are perceived either as deceptive performers or as producers of some undesirable discourse: be it bad drama, bad poetry, false letters, anti-feminist tracts, pro-Catholic books, or newsbooks. This interest in text and performance is linked with a wider concern in these plays about the definition of comic drama itself.

125

For reasons discussed in the Introduction, this study starts with the emergence of comical satire in 1599, at which point a dichotomy between text and performance is clear. *Poetaster* is the best example of a play which made an unproblematised division between wicked theatrical performance and virtuous text such as itself, while conversely *Satiromastix* mocked textuality and praised performance without worrying too much about how the two categories might overlap. Subsequent comic drama, although still taking one side or another of this dichotomy (*The Whore of Babylon, The Roaring Girl*) gradually problematised it until in plays like *A Game at Chess* and *The Staple of News* the two categories began to overlap and merge. By the 1630s, a synthesis had emerged in which "comic laws" could be both warrants of literary worth and guarantees of playhouse success. This idea was used against the court dramatists such as Suckling and Davenant—whose vision of the theatre was simply as another arena available for experimentation by courtly writers, albeit one cursed with an unpredictable and uncultured audience—in another row about the nature and future of professional theatre, whose effects were still being felt after the Restoration.

In short, personally satirical comedies are not, as they have previously been considered, a backwater of Renaissance drama, interesting mainly as biographical curiosities: they are the place where struggles about the nature, status, and future of professional drama are enacted, struggles that have conditioned critical paradigms of drama ever since.

NOTES

INTRODUCTION

1 All citations of Jonson, unless otherwise indicated, are from *Ben Jonson*, ed. C. H. Herford, Percy Simpson, and Evelyn Simpson, 11 vols. (Oxford: Clarendon P, 1925-51), henceforth H&S. See H&S IX.400 for a table of rival "identifications" within *Every Man Out.*

2 *Amazons and Warrior Women: Varieties of Feminism in Seventeenth-Century Drama* (Brighton: Harvester P, 1981) 212-14.

3 Anonymous biographer of Thomas Sutton, quoted in Robert C. Evans, *Jonson and the Contexts of his Time* (Lewisburg: Bucknell UP, 1994) 53. For representations of James I, see Julia Gasper, *The Dragon and the Dove: The Plays of Thomas Dekker* (Oxford: Clarendon P, 1990).

4 J. W. Bennett, "Oxford and *Endimion*," *PMLA* 57 (1942): 354-69.

5 Cf. Robert C. Evans, *Ben Jonson and the Poetics of Patronage* (Lewisburg: Associated University P, 1989); Evans, *Jonson and the Contexts of his Time*; Richard Dutton, *Mastering the Revels: The Regulation and Censorship of Renaissance Drama* (London: Macmillan, 1991); Dutton, *Ben Jonson: Authority: Criticism* (London: Macmillan, 1996).

6 *The Cornucopian Text: Problems of Writing in the French Renaissance* (Oxford: Clarendon P, 1979).

7 Stephen Gosson, *Markets of Bawdrie: The Dramatic Criticism of Stephen Gosson*, ed. Arthur F. Kinney (Salzburg: Salzburg UP, 1974) 165. See Kinney's Introduction, 65, for an account of antitheatrical literature in the twenty years following Gosson; also Jonas Barish, *The Antitheatrical Prejudice* (Berkeley: California UP, 1981) 116-19.

8 Gosson, *Markets of Bawdrie* 167.

9 On Aristophanes' profile in the Renaissance, see T. W. Baldwin, *Shakspere's smalle Latine and lesse Greeke*, 2 vols. (Urbana: Illinois UP, 1944); R. R. Bolgar, *The Classical Heritage and its Beneficiaries* (Cambridge: Cambridge UP, 1954); B. R. Smith, *Ancient Scripts and Modern Experience on the English Stage 1500-1700* (Princeton: Princeton UP, 1988). Aristophanes was available in Latin translation, but not in English, and was a set text in universities and occasionally in schools.

10 Lodge, *Defence of Poetry*, in *Elizabethan Critical Essays* ed. G. G. Smith, 2 vols. (1904; Oxford: Clarendon P, 1950) I.81-82: cf. Horace, *Satires* I.4.1-5.

11 See the Introduction to John Lyly, *Collected Works*, ed. R. W. Bond, 3 vols. (Oxford: Clarendon P, 1902); Bennett, "Oxford and *Endimion*." Sceptics include G. K. Hunter, *John Lyly: The Humanist as Courtier* (London: Routledge, 1962) and Carter A. Daniel, ed., *The Plays of John Lyly* (Lewisburg: Bucknell UP, 1988). On *Love's Labour's Lost*, see Frances A. Yates, *A Study of "Love's Labour's Lost"* (Cambridge: Cambridge UP, 1936); *Love's Labour's Lost*, ed. Richard David (London: Methuen, 1951) xvi-xvii, xxxvii-li; sceptical editors include G. R. Hibbard (Oxford: Clarendon P, 1990) 49-57, and John Kerrigan (Harmondsworth: Penguin, 1982) 9-10.

12 On Marprelate, the standard reference work remains William Pierce, *A Historical Introduction to the Marprelate Tracts: A Chapter in the Evolution of Religious and Civil Liberty in England* (London: Archibald Constable, 1908). Much Marprelate criticism remains

devoted to the authorship question; but see Raymond A. Anselment, *"Betwixt Jest and Earnest": Marprelate, Milton, Marvell, Swift and the Decorum of Religious Ridicule* (Toronto: Toronto UP, 1979). For "Martinomania," and the contemporary use of Old Comedy as a critical touchstone, see Matthew Steggle, "A New Marprelate Allusion," *Notes and Queries* 242 (1997): 34-36.

13 See O. J. Campbell, *Comicall Satyre and Shakespeare's "Troilus and Cressida"* (San Marino: Huntington Library, 1938).

14 *The Social Relations of Jonson's Theater* (Cambridge: Cambridge UP, 1992) 26-33.

15 *Forms of Nationhood: The Elizabethan Writing of England* (Chicago: Chicago UP, 1992), Chapter 5, "Staging Exclusion," 195-245; passage quoted, 226. On Armin, an Erasmian intellectual of a clown, and on his surviving works, see Muriel Bradbrook, *Shakespeare the Craftsman: The Clark Lectures 1968* (Cambridge: Cambridge UP, 1979) 49-74.

16 E. K. Chambers, *The Elizabethan Stage*, 4 vols. (Oxford: Clarendon P, 1923) I.322.

17 Chambers, *The Elizabethan Stage* I.324-25.

18 Chambers, *The Elizabethan Stage* I.324.

19 *The Whipping of the Satyre* lines 625-26 in *The Whipper Pamphlets*, ed. Arnold Davenport (Liverpool: Liverpool UP, 1951); cf. H&S IX.331-33. Mention should also be made of Jonson's problematic early comedy *The Case is Altered*, which caricatures Anthony Munday in the walk-on part of Antonio Balladino, an inept writer. The dating is uncertain, but it is clear that here too Jonson uses personation for polemic about the nature of good literature and drama; see H&S IX.308-9.

CHAPTER ONE

1 *Satiromastix*, Preface 8-9, cited from *The Dramatic Works of Thomas Dekker*, ed. Fredson Bowers, 4 vols. (Cambridge, 1955-1968); *OED* s.v. "poetomachia."

2 Unlike the "rediscovered" satirical intent of *Love's Labour's Lost*, *Satiromastix'* personal satire has been undisputed since the earliest historians of English drama: cf. Gerard Langbaine, *An Account of the English Dramatick Poets* (London, 1691) 121.

3 William Gifford, ed., *The Works of Ben Jonson, with a Memoir* (1816; London: Routledge, 1869) 13-14, 18.

4 Roscoe A. Small, *The Stage-Quarrel between Ben Jonson and the so-called Poetasters* (Breslau: M. & H. Marcus, 1899); Campbell, *Comicall Satyre and Shakespeare's "Troilus and Cressida."*

5 Philip J. Finkelpearl, *John Marston of the Middle Temple* (Cambridge, MA: Harvard UP, 1969), followed by Michael Scott, *John Marston's Plays: Theme, Structure and Performance* (London: Macmillan, 1978), and George L. Geckle, *John Marston's Drama: Themes, Images, Sources* (Rutherford: Farleigh Dickinson UP, 1980). Reginald W. Ingram, *John Marston* (Boston: Twayne, 1978), however, does discuss the War.

6 Cyrus Hoy, *Introductions, Notes and Commentaries to Texts in "The Dramatic Works of Thomas Dekker,"* 4 vols. (Cambridge: Cambridge UP, 1980); Gasper, *The Dragon and the Dove.*

7 David Mann, *The Elizabethan Stage Player: Contemporary Stage Representations* (London: Routledge, 1991) 101-28: Haynes, *The Social Relations of Jonson's Theater* 44-90: James Bednarz, "Shakespeare's Purge of Jonson: The Literary Context of *Troilus and Cressida*," *Shakespeare Studies* 21 (1993): 175-213; James Shapiro, *Rival Playwrights: Jonson, Shakespeare, Marlowe* (New York: Columbia UP, 1991).

⁸ Approaches to "oppositional" techniques in Renaissance drama include G. E. Rowe, *Distinguishing Jonson: Imitation, Rivalry, and the Direction of a Dramatic Career* (Lincoln: Nebraska UP, 1988); Gary Taylor, "Forms of Opposition: Shakespeare and Middleton," *English Literary Renaissance* 24 (1994): 283-314.

⁹ Jonson, *Poetaster*, ed. Thomas Cain (Manchester: Manchester UP, 1995), Introduction 30-36.

¹⁰ Confusingly, there are three different works entitled *Histriomastix* around this period, all of which bear on the anti-theatrical debate: one is the play under discussion, another is a Latin university comedy from the 1620s, and the third is the enormous work by William Prynne that attacked the theatre in general.

¹¹ Jonson, *Poetaster*, ed. Cain, Introduction 28-36; Marston, *What You Will*, ed. M. R. Woodhead (Nottingham: Nottingham Drama Texts, 1980), which I cite for textual references below. I follow Hoy in assigning *Satiromastix* entirely to Thomas Dekker.

¹² John Suckling, "The Wits," line 20, in *The Works of Sir John Suckling: The Non-dramatic Works*, ed. Thomas Clayton (Oxford: Clarendon P, 1971).

¹³ H&S IX.46-47.

¹⁴ See Matthew Steggle, "Jonson's *Every Man Out* and Commentators on Terence," *Notes and Queries* 242 (1997): 525-26.

¹⁵ H&S IX.427; a more exact source still proves elusive, although Jonson has been shown to be drawing on Minturno later on—see H. L. Snuggs, "The Source of Jonson's Definition of Comedy," *Modern Language Notes* 65 (1950): 543-44.

¹⁶ Serious work on the reception of Aristophanes is overdue: see W. Suss, *Aristophanes und die Nachwelt* (Leipzig: Theodor Wercher, 1911); Louis E. Lord, *Aristophanes: His Plays and Influence* (London: George G. Harrap, 1925). For Frye, see his *Anatomy of Criticism: Four Essays* (Princeton: Princeton UP, 1957) esp. 43-45, 158-86. Frye-misled critics include Coburn S. Gum, *The Aristophanic Comedies of Ben Jonson: A Comparative Study of Jonson and Aristophanes* (The Hague: Mouton, 1969) and Alifki Lafkidou Dick, *Paideia through Laughter: Jonson's Aristophanic Appeal to Human Intelligence* (The Hague: Mouton, 1974). However, see Ben Jonson, *Four Comedies*, ed. Helen Ostovich (London: Longman, 1997), Introduction 8-10 for a more judicious account of Jonson's use of Aristophanic precedent.

¹⁷ Francis Meres, *Palladis Tamia* in G. G. Smith, ed. *Elizabethan Critical Essays* II.323. There is no reason to suppose this anything but a strictly anecdotal judgement, although fragments of Eupolis do survive—cf. *Poetae Comici Graeci*, ed. R. Kassell and C. Austin (Berlin: Walter de Gruyter, 1983) V.294-539.

¹⁸ *Every Man Out* III.vi.195-207; see Sidney's *Defence of Poetry* in *The Miscellaneous Prose of Sir Philip Sidney*, ed. Katherine Duncan-Jones and Jan Van Dorsten (Oxford: Clarendon P, 1973) 113.

¹⁹ William Shakespeare, *Hamlet*, ed. G. R. Hibbard (Oxford: Clarendon P, 1987) II.ii.514, where Hamlet calls the players "the abstracts and brief chronicles of the time." *Hamlet*, of course, goes out of its way to allude to the contemporary vogue for comical satire, while at the same time Hamlet is busy trying to get a play to represent real people.

²⁰ Verbal echoes are traced by H&S IX.449-50.

²¹ H&S IX.404-6; Jasper Mayne, "To the Memory of Ben Jonson" lines 119-26 in H&S XI.454.

[22] E. A. G. Honigmann, *John Weever: A Biography of a Literary Associate of Shakespeare and Jonson* (Manchester: Manchester UP, 1995), 42-49. Points of similarity include short stature, love of tobacco, and alleged effeminacy.

[23] On Chester, see H&S IX.404-6; Charles Nicholl, *A Cup of News: The Life of Thomas Nashe* (London: RKP, 1984) 103-6; Matthew Steggle, "Charles Chester and Ben Jonson," *Studies in English Literature 1500-1900* (forthcoming 1999).

[24] H&S III.602 (Appendix X).

[25] Helen Ostovich, "'So Sudden and Strange a Cure': A Rudimentary Masque in *Every Man Out of his Humour*," *English Literary Renaissance* 22 (1992): 315-32.

[26] Jonas Barish, *Ben Jonson and the Language of Prose Comedy* (Cambridge, Mass.: Harvard UP, 1960) 113-21.

[27] See H&S I.406-12 for a summary of the ways in which the gallants might resemble their models.

[28] Cf. W. David Kay, *Ben Jonson: A Literary Life* (London: Macmillan, 1995) 27.

[29] See IV.v.11-12; V.vii; V.ix; IV.iii. Hedon also writes poetry: IV.iii.244-45.

[30] Jackson Cope, *The Theater and The Dream: from Metaphor to Form in Renaissance Drama* (Baltimore: Johns Hopkins UP, 1973); Robert N. Watson, *Ben Jonson's Parodic Strategy: Literary Imperialism in the Comedies* (Cambridge, Mass.: Harvard UP, 1987) 3.

[31] IV.ii.34. Also Amorphus, on his very first appearance, is described as "some trauailing motion" (I.iii.8).

[32] Sidney, *Miscellaneous Prose* 96.

[33] Gosson, *Markets of Bawdrie* 192.

[34] Sidney, *Miscellaneous Prose* 115. *As You Like It* was written around 1599-1600, *Twelfth Night* in 1601, the year after Jonson's play. Clearly such characters are in vogue as Jonson is writing *Cynthia's Revels*.

[35] Sidney, *Miscellaneous Prose* 95.

[36] Induction 33-37; see Richard Dutton, *Ben Jonson: to the First Folio* (Cambridge: Cambridge UP, 1983) 52. The imagery of the cockatrice is used to describe players by antitheatrical writers such as Stephen Gosson (*Markets of Bawdrie* 90), except that in Gosson they look *from* the stage *at* the audience.

[37] Induction 25: "secrecy" as a privileging device in Jonson has been studied by William W. E. Slights, *Ben Jonson and the Art of Secrecy* (Toronto: Toronto UP, 1994) esp. 144ff.

[38] Sidney, *Miscellaneous Prose* 120. The *OED* is not aware of any uses of it earlier than Sidney.

[39] *Poetaster* V.iii.77. See *OED* s.v. "commenter" for the evidence of its specifically classical reference.

[40] To which, the Author confesses in Apologetical Dialogue 141-47, arguing perversely that in this case people are mistaking genuinely *ad hominem* attacks for general slurs.

[41] Lodge, *Defence* in G. G. Smith, ed., *Elizabethan Critical Essays* I.81-82: cf. Horace *Satires* I.4.1-5.

[42] V.iii.305: see V.iii.34-37 for another allusion to Horace as a writer of humours.

CHAPTER TWO

[1] *What You Will* 520 (Lampatho threatens to write a satire against Quadratus); 1142 (Lampatho refers to the popularity of satirical comedies); 1555 (Quadratus says Lampatho might put him in a satirical comedy); 1915 (Quadratus wishes that Simplicius might be satirised in a comedy).

[2] Finkelpearl, *John Marston* 162-77; Anthony Caputi, *John Marston, Satirist* (Ithaca: Cornell UP, 1961) 156-78, quotation from 169: Richard A. Levin, "The Proof of the Parody," *Essays in Criticism* 24 (1974): 312-16.

[3] Jonson, *Conversations* 285-86; H&S I.140.

[4] Josiah H. Penniman, *The War of the Theatres* (Boston: Ginn, 1897) 137-43. The two characters certainly are similar in their social milieu and intellectual interests, leading to one description of Lampatho as a "teasing anamorphic double-portrait of the two rivals [Marston and Jonson]": *The Selected Plays of John Marston* ed. Macdonald P. Jackson and Michael Neill (Cambridge: Cambridge UP, 1986) Introduction xv.

[5] Finkelpearl, *John Marston* 163.

[6] John Taylor's elegy on Jonson, cited from H&S XI.425; *The Works of Ben Jonson*, ed. William Gifford, Introduction 3.

[7] *Cynthia's Revels*, III.ii.3,9,6; *Poetaster* Apologetical dialogue 213; *Satiromastix* I.ii.282, 309, I.ii.0 (stage direction).

[8] *Poetaster* IV.vii.24; *Satiromastix* I.ii.354.

[9] Finkelpearl, *John Marston* 163.

[10] Other similarities include Lampatho's "Jebusite" Catholicism; *What You Will* 514.

[11] *Cynthia's Revels* III.iii.18-23 (cf. also III.iii.26-27); *What You Will* 567-74.

[12] *The Cambridge History of Renaissance Philosophy*, ed. C. B. Schmitt and Quentin Skinner (Cambridge: Cambridge UP, 1988) 464ff. provides an excellent guide to the reinterpretation of Aristotle's theories in the Renaissance.

[13] *What You Will* 857-59. It is presumably through a profitable confusion with his namesake the heretic that Donatus here appears relegated to an incongruous "musty saw": an elegantly gratuitous dig at classical dramatic theory.

[14] *Poetaster*, Envy's Prologue 14-17; Hoy, I.179.

[15] H&S IX.535-36.

[16] Gasper, *The Dragon and the Dove*, 1.

[17] *Satiromastix*, To the World 54-55, 8, 27, 45. Even before the text proper starts, *Satiromastix* has appeared with a list of errata directed "Ad Lectorem," and a Latin quotation addressed "Ad Detractorem," both printed in Bowers' edition, I.306, 308.

[18] Jonson, *Poetaster* ed. Cain, Introduction 48-49.

[19] Cf. H&S IX.535: Hoy, I.188. Jonson's victim in *Every Man Out*, Charles Chester, had featured in *Skialetheia* under his own name, which also serves to suggest the closeness between verse satire and its dramatic equivalent: Everard Guilpin, *Skialetheia or a Shadowe of Truth, in Certaine Epigrams and Satyres*, ed. D. Allen Carroll (Chapel Hill: North Carolina UP, 1974), Satire II.47-51.

[20] The two exceptions are *What You Will*, which was not in print till 1607, and *Histriomastix* (1610).

[21] This point is argued by Hoy, I.183.

[22] *Satiromastix* II.ii.1-3, 11-14, 20. As Evans (*Ben Jonson and the Poetics of Patronage* 147) points out, this piece is specifically parodic of Jonson's patronage poems.

[23] This is the quarto text as it appears in the Bodleian copy, Malone 193 (1), for which H&S use the siglum B. Other quarto copies have readings that vary from this slightly, but not substantively; full details may be found in H&S's apparatus criticus at lines III.iii.8-10, 25-27.

[24] Alternatively, one would need to contest that they were a memorial transcription from an earlier performance of the play. Cf. Hoy I.197, 309-10 for transcriptions from a performance of *Satiromastix*: the standard of recall is, significantly, much lower in these examples than it is for Dekker's reproduction of Jonson.

[25] For a discussion of it there, and more generally of its other appearances in the thought of the period, see Stanley Fish, "Things and Actions Indifferent: The Temptation of Plot in *Paradise Regained*," *Milton Studies* 17 (1983): 163-86.

[26] See, e.g., I.ii.238-40, IV.i.157, IV.ii.182, IV.iii.178, V.ii.228, V.ii.323. And as Evans (*Jonson and the Contexts of his Time* 22-35) points out, another character too fond of oaths is King William himself.

[27] Jonson, *Discoveries* 2677; *Bartholomew Fair*, Induction 106; Hoy I.195. Previously it had been assumed that Dekker was merely being prophetic.

[28] See, for example, *Volpone* Dedication 57: "Where haue I beene particular? Where personall? except to a mimick, cheater, bawd or buffon, creatures (for their insolencies) fit to be tax'd?" Or, *Cynthia's Revels* III.iv.20, where he brackets together "mimiques, jesters, pandars, parasites."

[29] *OED* s.v. "Stagirite": there is, however, a prior use by John Marston, in *The Scourge of Villanie* IV.99. See *The Poems of John Marston*, ed. Arnold Davenport (Liverpool: Liverpool UP, 1961).

[30] *Poetaster* Apologetical Dialogue 45, 48. Dekker, on the other hand, makes it clear in his preface that he welcomes audiences who enjoyed the first Tucca and now want to enjoy the second as well.

CHAPTER THREE

[1] *All Fools*, Prologue 13-19, in *The Plays of George Chapman: The Comedies*, ed. Allan Holaday and Michael Kiernan (Urbana: Illinois UP, 1970).

[2] What is known about *The Old Joiner of Aldgate* is contained in C. J. Sisson's classic account, *Lost Plays of Shakespeare's Age* (Cambridge: Cambridge UP, 1936), which also considers the evidence concerning the lost collaborative play *Keep The Widow Waking*, a personally satirical tragicomedy from 1624. On *The Old Joiner*, see also Reavely Gair, *The Children of Pauls: The Story of a Theater Company* (Cambridge: Cambridge UP, 1982). Interestingly, one of the main victims can be linked to Jonson and to Marston, with both of whom Chapman collaborated. Among those represented on stage was a suitor of Agnes Howe by the name of John Flasket, who was involved directly in the War of the Theaters as the printer of *The Whipping of the Satire* (1601), a pamphlet that attacked both Marston and Jonson.

[3] Cf. Hoy, II.249-51, and Allardyce Nicoll, "The Dramatic Portrait of George Chapman," *Philological Quarterly* 41 (1962): 216-28.

[4] John Day, *The Ile of Gvls*, ed. G. B. Harrison (London: The Shakespeare Association, 1936) A2r-A3v; see Introduction vi for the subsequent arrests.

5 Collected by Philip Finkelpearl, "'The Comedians Liberty': Censorship of the Jacobean Stage Reconsidered," *English Literary Renaissance* 16 (1986): 123-38.

6 Thomas Tomkis, *Lingua* (1607; repr. n.p.: Old English Drama Students' Fascimile Edition, 1913), H2v. The play again uses Aristophanes as a touchstone for contemporary satirical drama at D4v-E1r.

7 *An Apology For Actors (1612) by Thomas Heywood. A Refutation of the Apology for Actors (1615) by I. G.*, ed. Richard H. Perkinson (New York: Scholars' Facsimiles and Reprints, 1941). Heywood, F4r, quoting Horace, *Satires* I.4.1-5; I. G., 20.

8 William Winstanley, *The Lives of the Most Famous English Poets* (London: H. Clark, 1687) 137. Other details that link *The Whore of Babylon* to comedy include the plaudite at the end. Julia Gasper argues that the play belongs to an international neo-Latin genre of "comedia apocalyptica": *The Dragon and The Dove*, 62-108.

9 Citations of the play will be from *The Dramatic Works of Thomas Dekker*, ed. Fredson Bowers. The context of the Parry conspiracy is discussed by Marianne G. Riely in her edition of *The Whore of Babylon* (New York: Garland, 1980) 288-90. The Albanoys appears at III.ii.103ff; on Creichton, see *DNB*, and Hoy II.347-48. The kinsman appears in V.i and V.ii. For Neville, see *DNB*, and Lacey Baldwin Smith, *Treason in Tudor England: Politics and Paranoia* (London: Cape, 1986) 13-20. For Gallio, see C. Berton, *Dictionnaire des Cardinaux* (1857; Farnborough: Gregg, 1969) 952.

10 Riely, Introduction, 68-69; see *DNB* for Charles Howard's life.

11 Edmund Spenser, *Poetical Works*, ed. E. De Selincourt (1912; Oxford: Oxford UP, 1990) 407-8.

12 A remark normally interpreted biographically; see Riely, Introduction 23.

13 I.i.68-69. It puns of course on "gospel."

14 III.ii.145 (for the source, see Hoy II.349); IV.ii.121; V.ii.135. For the Third King, see II.ii.1-15. Cf. Jean E. Howard, *The Stage and Social Stuggle in Early Modern England* (London: Routledge, 1994) 49-57, for more on such antitheatrical imagery in the play.

15 Thomas Dekker and Thomas Middleton, *The Roaring Girl*, ed. P. A. Mulholland (Manchester: Manchester UP, 1987) III.iii.186-89.

16 For Garzoni, see *The Works of Thomas Nashe*, ed. R. B. McKerrow, 5 vols. (London: A. H. Bullen; Sidgwick & Jackson, 1904-10) V.140-41.

17 On Jacques' desire for this sort of satirist's liberty, see *As You Like It*, ed. Alan Brissenden (Oxford: Clarendon P, 1993) II.vii.58-60, and commentary *ad loc.* for various contemporary analogues.

18 I.ii.25, 33, 39, 87, 99, 141; II.i.148, 185. There is a brief note on annotation styles in M. B. Parkes, *Pause and Effect* (Cambridge: Scolar P, 1992) 259-61; on Jonson's *Sejanus* quarto, see H&S IV.472ff.

19 Gosson, *Markets of Bawdrie* 86, 186, 192.

20 Mulholland, Introduction 23, shows how the pun on "venery" as "sexual activity" and as "trade" informs the play. And compare *The Whore of Babylon*'s preface, in which it is the actors who are reduced to tailors, cutting the fabric of a pre-existing woven text.

21 Simon Shepherd, *Amazons and Warrior Women* 74-83; Mary Beth Rose, "Women in Men's Clothing: Apparel and Social Stability in *The Roaring Girl*," *English Literary Renaissance* 14 (1984): 367-91; Jean E. Howard, *The Stage and Social Struggle* 121-27.

[22] Mulholland's commentary *ad loc.*; Gosson, *Markets of Bawdrie* 175; Deut. 22:5.

[23] I.ii.6; see Mulholland, Introduction 9 for reasons why this scene appears to be by Dekker. See Andrew Gurr, *Playgoing in Shakespeare's London* (Cambridge: Cambridge UP, 1987) 215, 219, 221, for primary references to cutpurses, including the intriguing detail that an apprehended cutpurse might in fact be bound to one of the pillars of the stage and put on display during the play.

[24] III.iii.207-9, II.i.151; for the allusion to the butcher, see P. A. Mulholland, "The Date of *The Roaring Girl*," *Review of English Studies* 28 (1977): 27-8.

[25] IV.ii.135-38. Mulholland *ad loc.* offers primary references for playhouse flags.

[26] III.iii.180-83: cf. Mulholland, Introduction 46-48.

[27] Whether the Inns-of-Court men stood among the groundlings is unclear. Gurr (209), quoting Sir John Davies, associates them with private rooms; alternatively, as Gurr himself shows (222) from Dekker's *Gulls Hornbook*, they also hired stools for use on stage. Possibly, then, Moll and Trapdoor may be referring to young lawyers sitting on the stage as they shoulder past them.

[28] *The Roaring Girl*, ed. A. W. Gomme (London: Ernest Benn, 1976) Introduction xiv. The anonymous biography, *The Womans Champion: or the Strange Wonder* (London, 1662), does not allude to her appearance on stage.

[29] *The Roaring Girl* II.ii.179. The association was also made by the Consistory Court that tried Mary Frith for immodesty a few months later, where her participation in *The Roaring Girl* formed part of the charges of immodest conduct brought against her; see Appendix E (pp.262-264) of Mulholland's edition, and the reference in the Epilogue quoted below.

[30] *Swetnam the Woman-hater: The Controversy and the Play*, ed. Coryl Crandall (West Lafayette, Indiana: Purdue UP, 1969); also referred to is the edition of A. B. Grosart (N.p.: privately printed, 1880). A facsimile of the play, with a brief introduction, appeared in *Female Replies to Swetnam the Woman-Hater*, ed. Charles Butler (Bristol: Thoemmes P, 1995).

[31] The *Araignment* is cited from the critical edition of F. W. Van Heertum (Nijmegen: Cicero P, 1989). See her Introduction, 20-35, for Swetnam's biography. Swetnam's *The Schoole of the Noble & Worthy Science of Defence* (London, 1617) has never been reprinted and is cited from the Bodleian copy. For a discussion of this work in the context of the history of fencing, see J. D. Aylward, *The English Master of Arms from the Twelfth to the Twentieth Century* (London: Routledge, 1956) 79-85.

[32] Speght, Sowernam, and Munda are cited from the anthology edited by Simon Shepherd, *The Women's Sharp Revenge: Five Women's Pamphlets from the Renaissance* (London: Fourth Estate, 1985). See Crandall, Introduction 27-28, for what is known of the reception of the play.

[33] On Speght, see Barbara Kiefer Lewalski, *Writing Women in Renaissance England* (Cambridge, MA: Harvard UP, 1993) 153-178. On Sowernam, see Megan Matchinske, "Legislating 'Middle-Class' Morality in the Marriage Market: Ester Sowernam's *Ester hath hang'd Haman*," *English Literary Renaissance* 24 (1994): 154-83. On *Swetnam*, Simon Shepherd in *Amazons and Warrior Women* 203-17 considers the play's politics, both sexual and otherwise, while Linda Woodbridge, in *Women and the English Renaissance: Literature and the Nature of Womankind, 1540-1620* (Urbana: Illinois UP, 1984) 300-22, praises it for its humanity and feminism. See also Constance Jordan, "Gender and Justice in *Swetnam the Woman-hater*," *Renaissance Drama* 18 (1987): 149-69.

[34] Thus Crandall spells the name, although Woodbridge and others prefer the more etymologically correct "Misogynos"; the spelling of the name in the quarto is very erratic, suggesting the author did not know the Greek behind its derivation.

[35] [Juan de Flores], *Histoire de Aurelio, et Isabelle* (Brussels, 1608), offers a parallel text in French, Spanish, Italian and English. In this piece, Afranio (the misogynist) is not mentioned as a writer of books, but the issue of literacy still has a certain importance. The woman advocate locates men's power in their command of literacy: "You that haue the penne in the hande, you writte all that pleasethe you" (G8r). So the systematic characterisation of Swetnam as a writer is perhaps greatly expanding a small hint in the source.

[36] Crandall, 22-26, discusses the source and notes that de Flores' novelette, in its original version, was also a satire against a misogynist under his real name—a poet named Torrellas. Could the writer of *Swetnam* have been aware of this connection?

[37] *Swetnam* associates Joseph Swetnam with Bristol, which agrees with the legal documents in which he is mentioned (quoted by Van Heertum, Introduction 20) but disagrees with his self-description in the *Schoole of Defence*, which locates him very firmly at Plymouth; therefore, the anonymous writer's knowledge of Swetnam is more than just the sum of Swetnam's own texts.

[38] Cf. Stanley Wells and Gary Taylor with John Jowett and William Montgomery, *William Shakespeare: A Textual Companion* (Oxford: Clarendon P, 1987) 34-36, 42, 64.

[39] I.ii.62: Swetnam names himself at I.ii.7.

[40] IV.iii.8; V.i.301-2, 305, 309; however, I think Crandall's correction of Q "Niniuersitie" to "Vniversitie" is missing another joke stressing Swash's ignorance.

[41] Speght, 59; Speght, 59; Munda, 140.

[42] On the Red Bull, see Gurr, *Playgoing in Shakespeare's London* 165 ff.

[43] I.ii.152-58; Swetnam, *Araignment* 228. Other detailed verbal echoes are traced chapter and verse by Van Heertum and Crandall.

[44] *Swetnam*, ed. Grosart, Introduction xlv.

[45] III.ii.52, 64; III.iii.207. Cf. also V.ii.139, 142, 329, 349.

[46] Alternatively, Simon Shepherd in *Amazons and Warrior Women* (212 ff.) reads Lorenzo as a royal allegory: in that he is a younger son whose elder brother has died, he resembles Prince Charles; in that his Amazon disguise recalls Sidney's *Arcadia*, he looks back to the glories of Elizabeth's reign and offers a chance to restore them.

[47] Robert C. Evans in *Jonson and the Contexts of his Time* (22-30) puts together verbal parallels showing that in *Satiromastix* the actions of the weak king, and his reformation, echo the actions, and the eventual reformation, of the weak poet. Here the link between Atticus and Misogenos works in the same way, since the weakness of Atticus lies precisely in putting too much trust in words, as well as in misogyny. The sub-plot hence informs the main play.

[48] Algernon Charles Swinburne, *The Age of Shakespeare* (London: Chatto & Windus, 1908) 165-66.

[49] Thomas Middleton, *A Game at Chess*, ed. T. H. Howard-Hill (Manchester: Manchester UP, 1993). All citations of the play are from this edition. References to "Howard-Hill" are to its editorial matter. Scribal expansions in the matter quoted from the appendix have been silently normalised.

[50] Howard-Hill, Appendix 202, 200.

[51] See Howard-Hill, Introduction, 22-26 for a discussion. Cf. Chambers, *The Elizabethan Stage* I.325 for other references to personations of James I.

[52] Richard Dutton, *Mastering the Revels: The Regulation and Censorship of Renaissance Drama* (London: Macmillan, 1991) 237-46.

[53] Howard-Hill, Appendix, 205; Nashe, *Works* III.80; George Ruggles [attr.], *Club Law*, ed. G. C. Moore Smith (Cambridge: Cambridge UP, 1907) Introduction xxxix-xl.

[54] Howard-Hill, Appendix 198, 201, 202, 202, 211.

[55] Howard-Hill, Appendix 204, 193.

[56] Howard-Hill, Appendix 204.

[57] As well as the printed text, it is clear that the play also circulated extensively in manuscript; the six surviving MS copies, which show the play in different stages of development, are discussed by Howard-Hill, Introduction 2-10, 29-32, 49-52.

[58] Paul Yachnin, "*A Game at Chess* and Chess Allegory," *Studies in English Literature 1500-1900* 22 (1982): 317-30.

[59] Jerzy Limon, *Dangerous Matter: English Drama and Politics in 1623/24* (Cambridge: Cambridge UP, 1986) 101-24.

[60] I.i.299-307. For *The Staple of News*, see below.

[61] II.i.12, II.i.192, II.ii.216, III.i.33.

[62] Howard-Hill, Introduction 45.

[63] IV.ii.51, II.i.220, IV.ii.62, 65.

[64] A. A. Bromham, "Middleton's Cardinal of Milan," *Notes and Queries* 225 (1980): 155-57, makes a case that De Dominis is also glanced at in *More Dissemblers Besides Women*.

[65] Michael McCanles, *The Text of Sidney's Arcadian World* (Durham: Duke UP, 1989) 1-14.

[66] Thomas Middleton, *Five Plays*, ed. Bryan Loughrey and Neil Taylor (Harmondsworth: Penguin, 1988), Introduction xx.

[67] See III.iii.23ff., V.i.10-18, V.i.36-45.

[68] For a discussion of this trope as it pertains to *A Game at Chess*, see Swapan Chakravorty, *Society and Politics in the Plays of Thomas Middleton* (Oxford: Clarendon P, 1996) 167-70.

[69] See Chambers, *The Elizabethan Stage* I.323, IV.401. It has been suggested that a complaint by Thomas Scot about such continental plays satirising the British royal family, and inviting British dramatists to answer in kind, may lie behind *A Game at Chess*; see Margot Heinemann, *Puritanism and Theatre: Thomas Middleton and Oppositional Drama under the Early Stuarts* (Cambridge: Cambridge UP, 1980) 157.

[70] Sidney *Miscellaneous Prose* 96.

[71] William Prynne, *Histriomastix: The Player's Scourge* (London, 1633) 121, 124. See Martin Butler, "William Prynne and the Allegory of Middleton's *Game at Chess*," *Notes and Queries* 228 (1983): 53; T. H. Howard-Hill, "More on 'William Prynne and the Allegory of Middleton's *Game at Chess*,'" *Notes and Queries* 234 (1989): 349-51, is more cautious.

CHAPTER FOUR

1 I. C., "Ode to Ben Jonson Upon his Ode to Himself" lines 5-20 (H&S XI.336-37). R. D. Peterson investigates the history of the epigram alluded to in lines 14-16, and points out how Jonson applies it to other people in his own poems: *Imitation and Praise in the Poetry of Ben Jonson* (New Haven: Yale UP, 1971) 92-93. Other eulogists who use Aristophanes as a reference point for praise of Jonson include William Habington, Barton Holyday, Robert Waring, and Jasper Mayne; cf. H&S XI.447, 353, 454, 478.

2 *Discoveries* 2654-77 (H&S VIII.644). There are problems with using *Discoveries* as direct evidence of a Jonsonian artistic credo, however; for instance, the fact that much of the passage quoted above is taken from Heinsius. On *Discoveries'* connection with Heinsius, and the implications for the date of *Discoveries*, see Paul R. Sellin, *Daniel Heinsius and Stuart England* (Leiden: Leiden UP, 1968) 147-63.

3 Robert C. Evans, *Jonson and the Contexts of his Time* 45-61; *Volpone*, Dedication 54-58, 73-74. H&S (IX.680-82) survey and reject other, later, allegations of personal satire concerning the play. For a wider-ranging review of scholarly literature on Jonson's topicality, see Ian Donaldson, *Jonson's Magic Houses: Essays in Interpretation* (Oxford: Clarendon P, 1997) 125-43.

4 John Aubrey, *Brief Lives*, ed. O. L. Dick (1949; Harmondsworth: Penguin, 1962) 347; Evans 53, 194, quoting two anonymous manuscripts of the Restoration period. I normalise the style of Evans' quotations.

5 *Epicoene*, "Another [Prologue]" lines 9-10; Francis Beaumont, "Upon the Silent Woman" lines 9-14 (see H&S XI.324). For Dryden's story, cf. H&S I.188, II.70. H&S V.144-46 further complicates matters by showing how the references to cross-dressing and the Prince of Moldavia were aimed at Lady Arabella Stuart and led to further trouble.

6 For Mayne, see H&S XI.449-54. Cavendish is cited in H&S X.47; however, in her story, these ideas are suggested by supernatural spirits, who apologise for having forgotten who the other characters represented. Later efforts at identifying personal satire in the play can be found in *The Alchemist*, ed. C. M. Hathaway (New York: Henry Holt, 1903), Introduction 94-103. On a different tack, see J. T. McCullen, "Conference with the Queen of Fairies," *Studia Neophilologica* 23 (1950): 87-95, who discusses the connections between the fraud in the play and the contemporary law-case of Thomas Rogers, a former Middle Templar deluded by conmen into believing he would be vouchsafed an audience with the Queen of Fairies.

7 Bodleian MS Rawl. B 158, p. 179. A brief discussion of the manuscript may be found in Evans, *Jonson and the Contexts of his Time* 53, though he does not discuss the two references to *The Alchemist*. H&S (I.184) call this MS "quite untrustworthy," but for my purposes the MS is important, as it is recording an existing tradition.

8 David McPherson, "The Origins of Overdo: A Study in Jonsonian Invention," *Modern Language Quarterly* 37 (1976): 221-33.

9 John Selden, *Table Talk*, ed. Frederick Pollock (London: Quaritch, 1927) 119; cf. H&S X.213. H&S also discuss an attempt by Fleay to see Samuel Daniel in John Littlewit, II.147-48.

10 *Ungathered Verse* XXXIV. 60-61, 72. John M. Potter, "Old Comedy in *Bartholomew Fair*," *Criticism* 10 (1968): 290-99, makes the case for echoes of Aristophanes within the play: a case vitiated by his equation of Greek Old Comedy and Fryean Old Comedy.

11 Aristophanes, *Knights* 232; Liddell and Scott s.v. σκευοποιός.

[12] *Conversations* 409-15 (H&S I.143-44).

[13] See William Webbe in G. G. Smith, ed., *Elizabethan Critical Essays* I.249, and Sandra Billington, *Mock Kings in Mediaeval Society and Renaissance Drama* (Oxford: Clarendon P, 1991) 273.

[14] V.iii.111-15; cf. Aristophanes, *Wealth* 850-52.

[15] *Jonson and the Contexts of his Time* 62-94. Cf. Julie Sanders, "A Parody of Lord Chief Justice Popham in *The Devil is an Ass*," *Notes and Queries* 242 (1997): 528-30.

[16] There is a brief biography of Butter in *DNB*; the context is discussed by J. Frank, *The Beginnings of the English Newspaper 1620-1660* (Cambridge, MA: Harvard UP, 1961) 1-18. See also Joad Raymond, ed., *Making the News: An Anthology of the Newsbooks of Revolutionary England, 1641-1660* (Moreton-in-Marsh: Windrush P, 1993), Introduction 3-4. Frank and others have suggested parallels between Captain Cymbal and Captain Gainsford, another early newsbook writer who died shortly before *The Staple of News* appeared; but the differences, starting with the fact that we are explicitly told in the play that Gainsford is dead and his style is outmoded, make any parallels trivial compared to the Nathaniel Butter personation. H&S (II.185) report and discount speculation about Madrigal being based on George Wither.

[17] Frank, *The Beginnings of the English Newspaper* 8.

[18] But see Nathaniel's final line: "I despaire not to be *Master!*" (III.iii.57).

[19] Alexander Gill, "Uppon Ben Jonsons 'Magnettick Ladye'" lines 15-18 (H&S XI.346-48).

[20] *A Game at Chess* III.i.50; *Staple of News* III.ii.69.

[21] For circulation of playtexts in manuscript in the period, see Harold Love, *Scribal Publication in Seventeenth-Century England* (Oxford: Clarendon P, 1993) 65-70.

[22] III.ii.119: the word is used of Fame's supply of rumours. The image of the cornucopia has been identified by Terence Cave in *The Cornucopian Text* as one of those typical of Renaissance attempts to come to grips with the whole concept of copious discourse.

[23] Sarah Pearl, "Sounding to Present Occasions: Jonson's Masques of 1620-1625," *The Court Masque*, ed. David Lindley (Manchester: Manchester UP, 1984) 60-77; quotation from 74.

[24] I[ohn] D[avies], *A Scourge for Paper-persecutors, or, Paper's Complaint, Compil'd in Ruthfull Rimes, Against the Paper-spoylers of these Times* (London, 1625). In the 1625 edition Davies' poem, which first appeared in 1611 as part of *The Scourge of Folly*, has been augmented with a continuation by Abraham Holland. It is cited from the *Complete Works* of John Davies of Hereford, ed. A. B. Grosart, 2 vols. (Edinburgh: privately printed, 1878) II.75-81.

[25] See *Magnetic Lady*, Induction 121; Aristophanes, *Clouds* 560-62; H&S X.43. See E. E. Duncan-Jones, "Jonson's Queen Cis," *The Ben Jonson Journal* 3 (1996): 147-52, for a persuasive suggestion of personal satire in *The New Inn*.

CHAPTER FIVE

[1] Martin Butler, *Theatre and Crisis 1632-1642* (Cambridge: Cambridge UP, 1984). The phrase "second war of the theatres" appears to have been coined by R. J. Kaufmann, *Richard Brome: Caroline Playwright* (New York: Columbia UP, 1961) and has been repeated by several subsequent commentators.

2 Kevin Sharpe challenges this division in a study of court drama which takes issue with Butler: *Criticism and Compliment: The Politics of Literature in the England of Charles I* (Cambridge: Cambridge UP, 1987) esp. 31-35. However, as this chapter will show, Brome and others were definitely under the impression that such a division existed. See also Ira Clark's definition of the division in *Professional Playwrights: Massinger, Ford, Shirley and Brome* (Lexington: Kentucky UP, 1992) 1-5; also A. H. Tricomi, *Anticourt Drama in England 1603-1642* (Charlottesville: Virginia UP, 1989), and Richard Dutton, *Mastering the Revels.*

3 Clark, *Professional Playwrights* 4.

4 See Richard Burt, *Licensed by Authority: Ben Jonson and the Discourses of Censorship* (Ithaca: Cornell UP, 1993).

5 Suckling, *Non-dramatic Works,* Introduction xliv.

6 Martin Garrett, *"A Diamond, though set in horn": Philip Massinger's Attitude to Spectacle* (Salzburg: Salzburg UP, 1984) 261.

7 Gerald Eades Bentley, *The Jacobean and Caroline Stage,* 7 vols. (Oxford: Clarendon P, 1941-68) I.108-34. See these playwrights' biographies in vols. III, IV, and V. Other playwrights from this list who appear to have courtly connections include "Sir Cornelius Formido" and Arthur Wilson.

8 Mary Edmond, *Rare Sir William Davenant* (Manchester: Manchester UP, 1987) 32, 40; *The Just Italian* can be found in *The Works of Sir William D'Avenant,* ed. James Maidment and W. H. Logan, 5 vols. (Edinburgh: William Paterson, 1872) I.199-280.

9 Peter Beal, "Massinger at Bay: Unpublished Verses in a War of the Theatres," *Yearbook of English Studies* 10 (1980): 190-203; Massinger's "Prologue" line 15. All three poems discussed — "Prologue," "To my honored ffriend," and "A Charme for a Libeller" — are cited from Beal's edition in this article. *The Maid of Honour* is in *The Plays and Poems of Philip Massinger,* ed. Philip Edwards and Colin Gibson, 5 vols. (Oxford: Clarendon P, 1976), I.105-97; the dating is discussed at I.xxi, though without knowledge of the Prologue. The discovery of the Prologue may affect the dating of the play; see D. S. Lawless, "On the Date of Massinger's *The Maid of Honour,*" *Notes and Queries* 231 (1986): 391-92.

10 "To my honored ffriend" line 58.

11 "A Charme" (lines 93-94) alleges the Libeller himself earns money from drama; Martin Garrett, ed., *Massinger: The Critical Heritage* (London: Routledge, 1991), Introduction 4-7.

12 "A Charme" line 134; *The Maid of Honour* I.i.85. "A Charme" lines 130-31, 17, 100; *The Maid of Honour* I.i.72, 96.

13 *The Maid of Honour* II.v.27-28; "A Charme" line 142. *The Maid of Honour* I.i.100-5; "A Charme" line 138.

14 William Davenant, "To Endimion Porter" line 24, in *The Shorter Poems and Songs from the Plays and Masques,* ed. A. M. Gibbs (Oxford: Clarendon P, 1972). 52-53.

15 For Habington, West, and further references, see Colin Gibson, "Another Shot in the War of the Theatres (1630)," *Notes and Queries* 232 (1987): 308-9; for Shirley, see George Bas, "James Shirley et 'Th'untun'd Kennell,'" *Etudes Anglaises* 16 (1963): 11-22. For Heywood, see M. Grivelet, "Th'Untun'd Kennell: Note sur Thomas Heywood et le Théâtre sous Charles 1er," *Etudes Anglaises* 7 (1954): 101-6. The second half of Grivelet's article — seeking to demonstrate personal reference in Heywood's 1634 work *Love's Mistress, or the Queen's Masque* — is far less convincing.

139

[16] N. W. Bawcutt, ed., *The Control and Censorship of Caroline Drama: The Records of Sir Henry Herbert, Master of the Revels 1623-1673* (Oxford: Clarendon P, 1996) 117. The revised text of *The Ball* is in *The Dramatic Works and Poems of James Shirley*, ed. William Gifford, 6 vols. (1833; New York: Russell & Russell, 1966) III.1-91. For Herbert's admiration of Shirley, see III.95, III.185. Butler, *Theatre and Crisis* 229, 235-36 discusses personations of monopolists and aldermen in lost 1630s comedies and in satirical pamphlet dialogues that may reflect a development of the jig.

[17] *The Dramatic Works of Richard Brome*, 3 vols. (London: John Pearson, 1873) III.ix, III.xi. This edition being unlineated, references are by page numbers.

[18] *The Works of Sir John Suckling: The Plays*, ed. L. A. Beaurline (Oxford, 1971) 1-32.

[19] Beaurline, in Suckling's *Plays* (286), agrees.

[20] Richard Brome, "Upon Aglaura in Folio" lines 33-34, in Suckling, *Non-dramatic Works* 201-2. Another writer who took the occasion to attack Suckling over this publication was Thomas May.

[21] R. J. Kaufmann, *Richard Brome* 151-68; see also Butler, *Theatre and Crisis* 220-27; Clark, *Professional Playwrights* 163-64.

[22] Kaufmann, *Richard Brome* 164. See Suckling, *Non-dramatic Works* Introduction xxvii, for more up-to-date information on Suckling's life, which doesn't affect the validity of Kaufmann's identification.

[23] Thomas Rymer, ed., *Foedera* (London, 1744) XX.377-78; see Edmond, *Rare Sir William Davenant* 75-76. John Freehafer, "Brome, Suckling, and Davenant's Theatre Project of 1639," *Texas Studies in Literature and Language* 10 (1968): 367-83, identifies the site and investigates a network of connections with other theatrical documents of the period.

[24] Freehafer, 375-79; Dutton, *Mastering the Revels*. This incident falls outside Dutton's time period.

[25] *The Court Begger* 184, cited from Volume I of the anonymously edited 1873 edition of Brome's *Dramatic Works*. Reference is by page number as the edition is unlineated.

[26] Cf. for instance the Epilogue of *Satiromastix*, where Dekker invites Jonson to respond in kind.

[27] Freehafer 370.

[28] *The Court Begger* 266, except that I emend an obvious corruption by reading "The Muses' skill" instead of "The Muses kill."

[29] *The Court Begger* 271; Freehafer (372) traces just such a rumour about Suckling's *Aglaura*.

[30] The identification is made by Freehafer 367, 379-81.

[31] Suckling, *Non-dramatic Works*, Introduction lix-lxi.

[32] Freehafer (382) argues this might have been motivated by Davenant's personal dislike of Brome. Alternatively, it could be argued that Brome's style simply fitted the new theatre less well: certainly, *A Jovial Crew*, one of the few Brome plays to survive into the Restoration repertoire, only did so by becoming a comic opera.

WORKS CITED

I—PRIMARY TEXTS

Aristophanes. *Aristophanes.* Ed. and tr. Benjamin Bickley Rogers. 3 vols. London: Heinemann, 1924.

Aubrey, John. *Brief Lives.* Ed. O. L. Dick. 1949; Harmondsworth: Penguin, 1962.

Bodleian MS Rawlinson B 158.

Brome, Richard. *The Dramatic Works of Richard Brome,* 3 vols. London: John Pearson, 1873.

Butler, Charles, ed. *Female Replies to Swetnam the Woman-Hater.* Bristol: Thoemmes P, 1995.

Chapman, George. *The Plays of George Chapman: The Comedies.* Ed. Allan Holaday and Michael Kiernan. Urbana: Illinois UP, 1970.

Davenant, William. *The Works of Sir William D'Avenant.* Ed. James Maidment and W. H. Logan. 5 vols. Edinburgh: William Paterson, 1872.

———. *The Shorter Poems and Songs from the Plays and Masques.* Ed. A. M. Gibbs. Oxford: Clarendon P, 1972.

Davenport, Arnold, ed. *The Whipper Pamphlets.* Liverpool: Liverpool UP, 1951.

D[avies of Hereford], I[ohn]. *A Scourge for Paper-persecutors, or, Paper's Complaint, Compil'd in Ruthfull Rimes, Against the Paper-spoylers of these Times.* London, 1625.

Davies of Hereford, John. *Complete Works.* Ed. A. B. Grosart. 2 vols. Edinburgh: privately printed, 1878.

Day, John. *The Ile of Gvls.* Ed. G. B. Harrison. London: The Shakespeare Association, 1936.

Dekker, Thomas. *The Dramatic Works of Thomas Dekker.* Ed. Fredson Bowers. 4 vols. Cambridge: Cambridge UP, 1955-68.

———. *The Whore of Babylon.* Ed. Marianne G. Riely. New York: Garland, 1980.

———, and Thomas Middleton. *The Roaring Girl.* Ed. P. A. Mulholland. Manchester: Manchester UP, 1987.

———, and Thomas Middleton. *The Roaring Girl.* Ed. A. W. Gomme. London: Ernest Benn, 1976.

Elizabethan Critical Essays. Ed. G. G. Smith. 2 vols. 1904; Oxford: Clarendon P, 1950.

[Flores, Juan de]. *Histoire de Aurelio, et Isabelle.* Brussels, 1608.

Gosson, Stephen. *Markets of Bawdrie: The Dramatic Criticism of Stephen Gosson.* Ed. Arthur F. Kinney. Salzburg: Salzburg UP, 1974.

Guilpin, Everard. *Skialetheia or a Shadowe of Truth, in Certaine Epigrams and Satyres.* Ed. D. Allen Carroll. Chapel Hill: North Carolina UP, 1974.

Heywood, Thomas. *An Apology For Actors (1612) by Thomas Heywood. A Refutation of the Apology for Actors (1615) by I. G.* Ed. Richard H. Perkinson. New York: Scholars' Facsimiles and Reprints, 1941.

Horace. *Satires, Epistles and Ars Poetica.* Ed. and tr. H. R. Fairclough. London: Heinemann, 1942.

Jonson, Ben. *Ben Jonson.* Ed. C. H. Herford, Percy Simpson, and Evelyn Simpson. 11 vols. Oxford: Clarendon P, 1925-51.

———. *The Works of Ben Jonson, with a Memoir.* Ed. William Gifford. 1816; London: Routledge, 1869.

———. *Four Comedies.* Ed. Helen Ostovich. London: Longman, 1997.

———. *The Alchemist.* Ed. C. M. Hathaway. New York: Henry Holt, 1903.

———. *Poetaster.* Ed. Tom Cain. Manchester: Manchester UP, 1995.

Lyly, John. *Collected Works.* Ed. R. W. Bond. 3 vols. Oxford: Clarendon P, 1902.

———. *The Plays of John Lyly.* Ed. Carter A. Daniel. Lewisburg: Bucknell UP, 1988.

Marston, John. *The Selected Plays of John Marston.* Ed. Macdonald P. Jackson and Michael Neill. Cambridge: Cambridge UP, 1986.

———. *What You Will.* Ed. M. R. Woodhead. Nottingham: Nottingham Drama Texts, 1980.

———. *The Poems of John Marston.* Ed. Arnold Davenport. Liverpool: Liverpool UP, 1961.

Massinger, Philip. *The Plays and Poems of Philip Massinger.* Ed. Philip Edwards and Colin Gibson. 5 vols. Oxford: Clarendon P, 1976.

Middleton, Thomas. *A Game at Chess.* Ed. T. H. Howard-Hill. Manchester: Manchester UP, 1993.

———. *Five Plays.* Ed. Bryan Loughrey and Neil Taylor. Harmondsworth: Penguin, 1988.

Nashe, Thomas. *The Works of Thomas Nashe.* Ed. R. B. McKerrow. 5 vols. London: A. H. Bullen; Sidgwick & Jackson, 1904-10.

Poetae Comici Graeci. Ed. R. Kassell and C. Austin. Berlin: Walter de Gruyter, 1983.

Prynne, William. *Histriomastix: The Player's Scourge.* London, 1633.

Ruggles, George [attr.]. *Club Law.* Ed. G. C. Moore Smith. Cambridge: Cambridge UP, 1907.

Selden, John. *Table Talk.* Ed. Frederick Pollock. London: Quaritch, 1927.

Shakespeare, William. *As You Like It.* Ed. Alan Brissenden. Oxford: Clarendon P, 1993.

――――. *Hamlet.* Ed. G. R. Hibbard. Oxford: Clarendon P, 1987.

――――. *Love's Labour's Lost.* Ed. Richard David. London: Methuen, 1951.

――――. *Love's Labour's Lost.* Ed. G. R. Hibbard. Oxford: Clarendon P, 1990.

――――. *Love's Labour's Lost.* Ed. John Kerrigan. Harmondsworth: Penguin, 1982.

Shepherd, Simon, ed. *The Women's Sharp Revenge: Five Women's Pamphlets from the Renaissance.* London: Fourth Estate, 1985.

Shirley, James. *The Dramatic Works and Poems of James Shirley.* Ed. William Gifford. 6 vols. 1833; New York: Russell & Russell, 1966.

Sidney, Philip. *The Miscellaneous Prose of Sir Philip Sidney.* Ed. Katherine Duncan-Jones and Jan Van Dorsten. Oxford: Clarendon P, 1973.

Spenser, Edmund. *Poetical Works.* Ed. E. De Selincourt. 1912; Oxford: Oxford UP, 1990.

Suckling, John. *The Works of Sir John Suckling: The Non-dramatic Works.* Ed. Thomas Clayton. Oxford: Clarendon P, 1971.

Suckling, John. *The Works of Sir John Suckling: The Plays.* Ed. L. A. Beaurline. Oxford: Clarendon P, 1971.

Swetnam, Joseph. *The Araignment of Lewd, Idle, Froward and Unconstant Women.* Ed. F. W. Van Heertum. Nijmegen: Cicero Press, 1989.

――――. *The Schoole of the Noble & Worthy Science of Defence.* London, 1617.

Swetnam the Woman-hater. Ed. A. B. Grosart. n.pl.: privately printed, 1880.

Swetnam the Woman-hater: The Controversy and the Play. Ed. Coryl Crandall. West Lafayette, Indiana: Purdue UP, 1969.

Tomkis, Thomas. *Lingua.* 1607; n.p.: Old English Drama Students' Fascimile Edition, 1913.

Winstanley, William. *The Lives of the Most Famous English Poets.* London, 1687.

The Womans Champion: or the Strange Wonder. London, 1662.

II—SECONDARY SOURCES

Anselment, Raymond A. *"Betwixt Jest and Earnest": Marprelate, Milton, Marvell, Swift and the Decorum of Religious Ridicule.* Toronto: Toronto UP, 1979.

Aylward, J. D. *The English Master of Arms from the Twelfth to the Twentieth Century.* London: Routledge, 1956.

Baldwin, T. W. *Shakspere's smalle Latine and lesse Greeke.* 2 vols. Urbana: Illinois UP, 1944.

Barish, Jonas. *Ben Jonson and the Language of Prose Comedy.* Cambridge, Mass.: Harvard UP, 1960.

――――. *The Antitheatrical Prejudice.* Berkeley: California UP, 1981.

Bas, George. "James Shirley et 'Th'untun'd Kennell.'" *Etudes Anglaises* 16 (1963): 11-22.

Bawcutt, N. W., ed. *The Control and Censorship of Caroline Drama: The Records of Sir Henry Herbert, Master of the Revels 1623-1673*. Oxford: Clarendon P, 1996.

Beal, Peter. "Massinger at Bay: Unpublished Verses in a War of the Theatres." *Yearbook of English Studies* 10 (1980): 190-203.

Bednarz, James. "Shakespeare's Purge of Jonson: The Literary Context of *Troilus and Cressida*." *Shakespeare Studies* 21 (1993): 175-213.

Bennett, J. W. "Oxford and *Endimion*." *PMLA* 57 (1942): 354-69.

Bentley, Gerald Eades. *The Jacobean and Caroline Stage*. 7 vols. Oxford: Clarendon P, 1941-68.

Berton, C. *Dictionnaire des Cardinaux*. 1857; Farnborough: Gregg, 1969.

Billington, Sandra. *Mock Kings in Mediaeval Society and Renaissance Drama*. Oxford: Clarendon P, 1991.

Bolgar, R. R. *The Classical Heritage and its Beneficiaries*. Cambridge: Cambridge UP, 1954.

Bradbrook, Muriel. *Shakespeare the Craftsman: The Clark Lectures 1968*. Cambridge: Cambridge UP, 1979.

Bromham, A. A. "Middleton's Cardinal of Milan." *Notes and Queries* 225 (1980): 155-57.

Burt, Richard. *Licensed by Authority: Ben Jonson and the Discourses of Censorship*. Ithaca: Cornell UP, 1993.

Butler, Martin. *Theatre and Crisis 1632-1642*. Cambridge: Cambridge UP, 1984.

―――. "William Prynne and the Allegory of Middleton's *Game at Chess*." *Notes and Queries* 228 (1983): 53.

The Cambridge History of Renaissance Philosophy. Ed. C. B. Schmitt and Quentin Skinner. Cambridge: Cambridge UP, 1988.

Campbell, O. J. *Comicall Satyre and Shakespeare's "Troilus and Cressida."* San Marino: Huntington Library, 1938.

Caputi, Anthony. *John Marston, Satirist*. Ithaca: Cornell UP, 1961.

Cave, Terence. *The Cornucopian Text: Problems of Writing in the French Renaissance*. Oxford: Clarendon P, 1979.

Chakravorty, Swapan. *Society and Politics in the Plays of Thomas Middleton*. Oxford: Clarendon P, 1996.

Chambers, E. K. *The Elizabethan Stage*. 4 vols. Oxford: Clarendon P, 1923.

Clark, Ira. *Professional Playwrights: Massinger, Ford, Shirley and Brome*. Lexington: Kentucky UP, 1992.

Cope, Jackson I. *The Theater and The Dream: from Metaphor to Form in Renaissance Drama*. Baltimore: Johns Hopkins UP, 1973.

Dick, Alifki Lafkidou. *Paideia through Laughter: Jonson's Aristophanic Appeal to Human Intelligence*. The Hague: Mouton, 1974.

Donaldson, Ian. *Jonson's Magic Houses: Essays in Interpretation*. Oxford: Clarendon P, 1997.

Duncan-Jones, E. E. "Jonson's Queen Cis." *The Ben Jonson Journal* 3 (1996): 147-52.

Dutton, Richard. *Ben Jonson: to the First Folio*. Cambridge: Cambridge UP, 1983.

————. *Mastering the Revels: The Regulation and Censorship of Renaissance Drama*. London: Macmillan, 1991.

Edmond, Mary. *Rare Sir William Davenant*. Manchester: Manchester UP, 1987.

Evans, Robert C. *Ben Jonson and the Poetics of Patronage*. Lewisburg: Associated University P, 1989.

————. *Jonson and the Contexts of his Time*. Lewisburg: Bucknell UP, 1994.

Finkelpearl, Philip J. *John Marston of the Middle Temple*. Cambridge, Mass.: Harvard UP, 1969.

————. "'The Comedians Liberty': Censorship of the Jacobean Stage Reconsidered." *English Literary Renaissance* 16 (1986): 123-38.

Fish, Stanley. "Things and Actions Indifferent: The Temptation of Plot in *Paradise Regained*." *Milton Studies* 17 (1983): 163-86.

Frank, J. *The Beginnings of the English Newspaper 1620-1660*. Cambridge, Mass.: Harvard UP, 1961.

Freehafer, John. "Brome, Suckling, and Davenant's Theatre Project of 1639." *Texas Studies in Literature and Language* 10 (1968): 367-83.

Frye, Northrop. *Anatomy of Criticism: Four Essays*. Princeton: Princeton UP, 1957.

Gair, Reavely. *The Children of Pauls: The Story of a Theater Company*. Cambridge: Cambridge UP, 1982.

Garrett, Martin. *"A Diamond, though set in horn": Philip Massinger's Attitude to Spectacle*. Salzburg: Salzburg UP, 1984.

————, ed. *Massinger: The Critical Heritage*. London: Routledge, 1991.

Gasper, Julia. *The Dragon and the Dove: The Plays of Thomas Dekker*. Oxford: Clarendon P, 1990.

Geckle, George L. *John Marston's Drama: Themes, Images, Sources*. Rutherford: Farleigh Dickinson UP, 1980.

Gibson, Colin. "Another Shot in the War of the Theatres (1630)." *Notes and Queries* 232 (1987): 308-9.

Grivelet, M. "Th' Untun'd Kennell: Note sur Thomas Heywood et le Théâtre sous Charles 1er." *Etudes Anglaises* 7 (1954): 101-6.

Gum, Coburn S. *The Aristophanic Comedies of Ben Jonson: A Comparative Study of Jonson and Aristophanes.* The Hague: Mouton, 1969.

Gurr, Andrew. *Playgoing in Shakespeare's London.* Cambridge: Cambridge UP, 1987.

Haynes, Jonathan. *The Social Relations of Jonson's Theater.* Cambridge: Cambridge UP, 1992.

Heinemann, Margot. *Puritanism and Theatre: Thomas Middleton and Oppositional Drama under the Early Stuarts.* Cambridge: Cambridge UP, 1980.

Helgerson, Richard. *Forms of Nationhood: The Elizabethan Writing of England.* Chicago: Chicago UP, 1992.

Honigmann, E. A. G. *John Weever: A Biography of a Literary Associate of Shakespeare and Jonson.* Manchester: Manchester UP, 1987.

Howard, Jean E. *The Stage and Social Struggle in Early Modern England.* London: Routledge, 1994.

Howard-Hill, T. H. "More on 'William Prynne and the Allegory of Middleton's *Game at Chess.'*" *Notes and Queries* 234 (1989): 349-51.

Hoy, Cyrus. *Introductions, Notes and Commentaries to Texts in "The Dramatic Works of Thomas Dekker."* 4 vols. Cambridge: Cambridge UP, 1980.

Hunter, G. K. *John Lyly: The Humanist as Courtier.* London: Routledge, 1962.

Ingram, Reginald W. *John Marston.* Boston: Twayne, 1978.

Jordan, Constance. "Gender and Justice in *Swetnam the Woman-hater.*" *Renaissance Drama* 18 (1987): 149-69.

Kaufmann, R. J. *Richard Brome: Caroline Playwright.* New York: Columbia UP, 1961.

Kay, W. David. *Ben Jonson: A Literary Life.* London: Macmillan, 1995.

Langbaine, Gerard. *An Account of the English Dramatick Poets.* London, 1691.

Lawless, D. S. "On the Date of Massinger's *The Maid of Honour.*" *Notes and Queries* 231 (1986): 391-92.

Levin, Richard A. "The Proof of the Parody." *Essays in Criticism* 24 (1974): 312-16.

Lewalski, Barbara Kiefer. *Writing Women in Renaissance England.* Cambridge, Mass.: Harvard UP, 1993.

Limon, Jerzy. *Dangerous Matter: English Drama and Politics in 1623/24.* Cambridge: Cambridge UP, 1986.

Lord, Louis E. *Aristophanes: His Plays and Influence.* London: George G. Harrap, 1925.

Love, Harold. *Scribal Publication in Seventeenth-Century England.* Oxford: Clarendon P, 1993.

Mann, David. *The Elizabethan Stage Player: Contemporary Stage Representations.* London: Routledge, 1991.

Matchinske, Megan. "Legislating 'Middle-Class' Morality in the Marriage Market: Ester Sowernam's *Ester hath hang'd Haman*." *English Literary Renaissance* 24 (1994): 154-83.

McCanles, Michael. *The Text of Sidney's Arcadian World.* Durham: Duke UP, 1989.

McCullen, J. T. "Conference with the Queen of Fairies." *Studia Neophilologica* 23 (1950): 87-95.

McPherson, David. "The Origins of Overdo: A Study in Jonsonian Invention." *Modern Language Quarterly* 37 (1976): 221-33.

Mulholland, Paul A. "The Date of *The Roaring Girl.*" *Review of English Studies* 28 (1977): 27-28.

Nicholl, Charles. *A Cup of News: The Life of Thomas Nashe.* London: Routledge, 1984.

Nicoll, Allardyce. "The Dramatic Portrait of George Chapman." *Philological Quarterly* 41 (1962): 216-28.

Ostovich, Helen. "'So Sudden and Strange a Cure': A Rudimentary Masque in *Every Man Out of his Humour.*" *English Literary Renaissance* 22 (1992): 315-32.

Parkes, Malcolm B. *Pause and Effect.* Cambridge: Scolar P, 1992.

Pearl, Sarah. "Sounding to Present Occasions: Jonson's Masques of 1620-1625." *The Court Masque.* Ed. David Lindley. Manchester: Manchester UP, 1984. 60-77.

Penniman, Josiah H. *The War of the Theatres.* Boston: Ginn, 1897.

Petersen, Richard D. *Imitation and Praise in the Poetry of Ben Jonson.* New Haven: Yale UP, 1971.

Pierce, William. *A Historical Introduction to the Marprelate Tracts: A Chapter in the Evolution of Religious and Civil Liberty in England.* London: Archibald Constable, 1908.

Potter, John M. "Old Comedy in *Bartholomew Fair.*" *Criticism* 10 (1968): 290-99.

Raymond, Joad, ed. *Making the News: An Anthology of the Newsbooks of Revolutionary England, 1641-1660.* Moreton-in-Marsh: Windrush P, 1993.

Rose, Mary Beth. "Women in Men's Clothing: Apparel and Social Stability in *The Roaring Girl.*" *English Literary Renaissance* 14 (1984): 367-91.

Rowe, George E. *Distinguishing Jonson: Imitation, Rivalry, and the Direction of a Dramatic Career.* Lincoln: Nebraska UP, 1988.

Rymer, Thomas, ed. *Foedera.* London, 1744.

Sanders, Julie. "A Parody of Lord Chief Justice Popham in *The Devil is an Ass.*" *Notes and Queries* 242 (1997): 528-30.

Scott, Michael. *John Marston's Plays: Theme, Structure and Performance.* London: Macmillan, 1978.

Sellin, Paul R. *Daniel Heinsius and Stuart England.* Leiden: Leiden UP, 1968.

Shapiro, James. *Rival Playwrights: Jonson, Shakespeare, Marlowe.* New York: Columbia UP, 1991.

Sharpe, Kevin. *Criticism and Compliment: The Politics of Literature in the England of Charles I*. Cambridge: Cambridge UP, 1987.

Shepherd, Simon. *Amazons and Warrior Women: Varieties of Feminism in Seventeenth-Century Drama*. Brighton: Harvester P, 1981.

Sisson, C. J. *Lost Plays of Shakespeare's Age*. Cambridge: Cambridge UP, 1936.

Slights, William W. E. *Ben Jonson and the Art of Secrecy*. Toronto: Toronto UP, 1994.

Small, Roscoe A. *The Stage-Quarrel between Ben Jonson and the So-called Poetasters*. Breslau: M. & H. Marcus, 1899.

Smith, B. R. *Ancient Scripts and Modern Experience on the English Stage 1500-1700*. Princeton: Princeton UP, 1988.

Smith, Lacey Baldwin. *Treason in Tudor England: Politics and Paranoia*. London: Cape, 1986.

Snuggs, H. L. "The Source of Jonson's Definition of Comedy." *Modern Language Notes* 65 (1950): 543-44.

Steggle, Matthew. "A New Marprelate Allusion." *Notes and Queries* 242 (1997): 34-36.

———. "Charles Chester and Ben Jonson." *Studies in English Literature 1500-1900* (forthcoming 1999).

———. "Jonson's *Every Man Out* and Commentators on Terence." *Notes and Queries* 242 (1997): 525-26.

Swinburne, Algernon Charles. *The Age of Shakespeare*. London: Chatto & Windus, 1908.

Suss, W. *Aristophanes und die Nachwelt*. Leipzig: Theodor Wercher, 1911.

Taylor, Gary. "Forms of Opposition: Shakespeare and Middleton." *English Literary Renaissance* 24 (1994): 283-314.

Tricomi, Arthur H. *Anticourt Drama in England 1603-1642*. Charlottesville: Virginia UP, 1989.

Watson, Robert N. *Ben Jonson's Parodic Strategy: Literary Imperialism in the Comedies*. Cambridge, Mass.: Harvard UP, 1987.

Wells, Stanley, and Gary Taylor, with John Jowett and William Montgomery. *William Shakespeare: A Textual Companion*. Oxford: Clarendon P, 1987.

Woodbridge, Linda. *Women and the English Renaissance: Literature and the Nature of Womankind, 1540-1620*. Urbana: Illinois UP, 1984.

Yachnin, Paul. "*A Game at Chess* and Chess Allegory." *Studies in English Literature 1500-1900* 22 (1982): 317-30.

Yates, Frances A. *A Study of "Love's Labour's Lost."* Cambridge: Cambridge UP, 1936.

ENGLISH LITERARY STUDIES MONOGRAPH SERIES

ENGLISH LITERARY STUDIES publishes peer-reviewed monographs (usual length, 45,000-60,000 words) on the literatures written in English. The Series is open to a wide range of scholarly and critical methodologies, and it considers for publication bibliographies, scholarly editions, and historical and critical studies of significant authors, texts, and issues. ELS publishes two to five monographs annually.